*The Stuff of Our Forebears*
WILLA CATHER'S SOUTHERN HERITAGE

T0308087

# The Stuff of Our Forebears

## Willa Cather's Southern Heritage

Joyce McDonald

THE UNIVERSITY OF ALABAMA PRESS

*Tuscaloosa*

The University of Alabama Press
Tuscaloosa, Alabama 35487-0380
uapress.ua.edu

Hardcover edition published 1998.
Paperback edition published 2019.
eBook edition published 2019.

Cover design: Lucinda Smith

Paperback ISBN: 978-0-8173-5958-4
eBook ISBN: eBook 978-0-8173-9264-2

A previous edition of this book has been catalogued by the Library of Congress
as follows:

Library of Congress Cataloging-in-Publication Data

McDonald, Joyce.
The stuff of our forebears: Willa Cather's Southern heritage /
Joyce McDonald.
    p.   c.m.
Includes bibliographical references (p.   ) and index.
ISBN 0-8173-0920-9
1. Cather, Willa, 1873–1947—Knowledge—Southern States. 2. Women
and literature—Southern States—History—20th century. 3. Pastoral ficton,
American—History and criticism. 4. Southern States—In literature. 5. Country
life in literature. I. Title
PS3505.A87Z737    1998
813'.52—dc21        97-40646
British Library Cataloguing-in-Publication data available

*For my father*
*Eugene William Schanbacher*

# Contents

# Preface

My interest in the effects of Willa Cather's Virginia background on her canon arose from, among other things, my interest in sociocultural influences. My husband was born and raised in the South, and although he left home at age eighteen and has resided in the Northeast for most of his adult life, he is still in many ways a Southerner. Why then, I wondered, would Cather not have retained much of her own heritage, particularly since those early influences were part of her formative years. Cather not only spent the first nine and a half years of her life in Back Creek, Virginia, but even on the Nebraska plains she was surrounded by her Southern family. In addition to her immediate family, Cather's paternal grandparents, maternal grandmother, and her Aunt Franc and Uncle George Cather had also relocated to Nebraska. Moreover, many Virginians from the Winchester area, where the Cathers had resided for generations, also chose to migrate West following the Civil War. The area of Nebraska in which they settled was often referred to as New Virginia. The point, of course, is that the South went with Cather to Nebraska and continued to influence her in subtle ways, not only during those Midwest years but throughout her life.

One's cultural heritage, that complex network of shared assumptions that bind a given society together, is not easily dismissed. Willa Cather may have rebelled against her mother's genteel traditions, and she may have chosen to ignore her Southern roots, but ultimately the influence of those early years prevailed. We see it in the class consciousness and aesthetic sensibility of her characters and in their sense of place and desire for historical continuity. We also find it in Cather's narrative technique of weaving stories within stories and in her use of folklore. But what most links Cather to the South and to the Southern literary tradition is her use of pastoral modes.

My contention that Willa Cather's versions of the pastoral are a
product of her Southern sensibility and share common factors with the
Southern literary tradition is supported by sequential analytical readings
of seven of her novels with occasional allusions and references to her
other works. Further support for my study comes from the many excel-
lent biographical works that detail Cather's early years in Virginia, her
relationship to her antebellum parents and grandmother, and their influence on her literary vision.

While I occasionally allude to Southern writers from the antebellum
and postbellum eras[1] and suggest parallel stages between Cather's work
and the work of Southern authors, this is not a comparative study. My
intention is not to explore in depth those possible literary influences and
connections but rather to show how the cultural influences Cather shares
with these authors have led them in similar directions.

I have used the term *aristocrat* rather than *plutocrat* when discussing
many of Cather's characters (although I am aware the term perpetuates
one of the myths of the Old South) because I believe the choice reflects
Cather's intent, which is to convey a particular state of mind, or elitist
world view, an artistic sensibility that shuns crass materialism. This perspective views money as the means to cultural refinement and good taste
rather than to mere consumerism.

Willa Cather has often been criticized for her indifference to social
activism.[2] But during her esteemed career Cather's novels often dealt
with small-town prejudices against minority groups, championed tolerance and understanding of other religions and cultures, and above all,
challenged readers to contemplate more than one side of an issue. And
although she was not given to supporting social causes for particular
groups, she was undiscriminatingly and fiercely loyal to her friends—
people from all classes and religions. She often sent gifts and money to
help support the drought-plagued Nebraska immigrant farmers she had
known and loved as a child, while choosing to live within relatively mod-
est means.

But Willa Cather's first loyalty was always to her art. When accused
by critics of writing about the past as a form of escapist art, she replied,
"What has art ever been but escape? . . . the world has a habit of being
in a bad way from time to time, and art has never contributed anything
to help matters—except escape" (*WCW* 18–19). Some may seek to change

the wrongs of the world through political and social channels. But when the world is "being in a bad way," we might also gratefully turn to those who would offer us an imaginary sanctuary from the chaos and confusion; to this end, Willa Cather has succeeded beyond measure.

# *Acknowledgments*

I am greatly indebted to a number of people who were instrumental in the completion of this book. My deepest gratitude goes to Merrill Maguire Skaggs for her generous encouragement and expert direction. Special thanks are also extended to Bruce Baker, John J. Murphy, Jo Ann Middleton, and Joan Weimer for their insightful readings and suggestions. In addition I would like to thank James Woodress for his prompt and helpful replies to my queries.

I could not have completed my research without the generous assistance of the library staff at the Rose Memorial Library, Drew University; the staff of the Willa Cather Historical Museum; Cynthia Hamilton, librarian at the Jaffrey Public Library; and Susan and David Parry, current owners of Willow Shade.

Deep appreciation also goes to my parents Mayme and Eugene Schanbacher, who instilled in me a love for literature and an interest in history at an early age. Finally, I extend my most heartfelt gratitude to my husband, Dwaine, born and raised in the South, who, in sharing his own personal history over the years, led me to wonder about Willa Cather's Southern roots.

# *Abbreviations*

| | |
|---|---|
| *ATOP* | *April Twilights and Other Poems* (1923 edition) |
| *CSF* | *Willa Cather's Collected Short Fiction, 1892–1912*, ed. Virginia Faulkner |
| *DCA* | *Death Comes for the Archbishop* |
| *KA* | *The Kingdom of Art*, ed. Bernice Slote |
| *MA* | *My Ántonia* |
| *MME* | *My Mortal Enemy* |
| *OD* | *Obscure Destinies* |
| *SSG* | *Sapphira and the Slave Girl* |
| *WCP* | *Willa Cather in Person: Interviews, Speeches, and Letters*, ed. L. Brent Bohlke |
| *WCW* | *Willa Cather on Writing* |
| *WP* | *The World and the Parish: Willa Cather's Articles and Reviews, 1893–1902*, ed. William M. Curtin |

## The Stuff of Our Forebears
### WILLA CATHER'S SOUTHERN HERITAGE

" . . . as we grow old we become more and more the stuff our
forebears put into us."

—from *My Mortal Enemy*

# Introduction

In an 1894 review of a production of *Uncle Tom's Cabin,* Willa Cather readily, if not objectively, rose to the defense of her Southern heritage, calling the play "exaggerated, overdrawn, abounding in facts but lacking in truth," much like the book (*KA* 269). She further reproached the author, Harriet Beecher Stowe, whom she envisioned sitting "under cold skies of the north," for attempting "to write of one of the warmest, richest and most highly-colored civilizations the world has ever known" (270). Although Cather ostensibly eschewed social activism and political issues, she nevertheless took a rare stand on this obviously personal and highly charged political issue.

Yet, true to her contradictory nature, Willa Cather could also be extremely critical of the South, revealing a marked "distaste for the polite conventions and ritual blather of genteel southern society."[1] During a 1913 visit to her birthplace, Gore, Virginia (formerly Back Creek), she wrote Elizabeth Shepley Sergeant that she found the men cowed and broken, and particularly "disliked the romantic Southern attitude."[2] Although Cather did not specifically qualify what this attitude might be, we may assume she was referring to the postbellum myths such as the Cavalier legend and the plantation pastorals that were so popular with both the North and South after the Civil War. Apparently she had long since forgotten her own romantic visions of that "highly-colored civili-

1

zation." On her third and final trip to Virginia she remarked to her life-long companion Edith Lewis that the acacia trees "had the shiftless look that characterized so many Southern things," but then added, in a typical Catherian reversal, that the wood of these trees "was the toughest of all."[3] Perhaps this last example best signifies Cather's own ambivalence toward her Southern heritage.

At times Cather does appear to disregard the influence of these early years, focusing instead on the time she spent in Nebraska. In an oft-quoted interview she stated "the years from 8 to 15 are the formative period of a writer's life, when he unconsciously gathers basic material" (*WCP* 31). Since Cather's family moved to Nebraska when she was nine, her statement does seem to suggest she saw little or no literary value in her Virginia childhood.[4] As noted by Elizabeth Shepley Sergeant, Mildred Bennett, and others, however, Cather related that those experiences which made the deepest impression on her came before she was twenty, suggesting those first nine years spent in the South were influential. Moreover, the interview in which Cather refers to the ages of eight to fifteen as a writer's formative years appeared in the *Omaha Bee*, a Nebraska newspaper. Willa Cather's ostensible "dismissal" of those early Virginia years may have been nothing more than a desire to emphasize her Nebraska childhood experience for the benefit of her Nebraska audience. When the interview appeared in 1921, all of Cather's novels, with the exception of the first, *Alexander's Bridge*, had been set on the western prairie in either Nebraska or Colorado. To credit her early Nebraska memories (which actually began when she was almost ten) is certainly a valid reason for highlighting those particular years. But whether she intended the statement as a dismissal of her Virginia childhood is questionable.

Like most Southern writers, Cather had a strong sense of place. Constantly associated with the Nebraska plains, she often expressed her displeasure at being considered a regional writer. Nevertheless, her instinct was toward the regional rather than the national. Although she depicted landscapes from different parts of the nation, her deep sense of place— usually attributed to Southern writers—dominated much of her work.[5] "She did not come out of Virginia for nothing," Eudora Welty wrote. "She saw the landscape had mystery as well as reality."[6]

For Cather, the land was a living, breathing entity. Edith Lewis tells us Cather "saw the country, not as pure landscape, but filled with a human significance, lightened or darkened by the play of human feeling."[7] Welty, a Southerner herself, seems to take Cather's Southern heritage, and its connection to her work, for granted, comparing Cather to William Faulkner, "another writer of Southern origin,"[8] who like Cather, sought continuity through place and history. Bernice Slote confirms the continuity of Cather's sense of place by pointing out that the landscape in her early short story "The Elopement of Allen Poole" is the same landscape Cather would duplicate forty-seven years later in *Sapphira and the Slave Girl.*[9]

Place, as Welty suggests, affords the writer a sense of history and continuity. Moreover, as the fictional works of numerous antebellum and postbellum writers reveal, history and the pastoral are inexorably intertwined in the Southern literary imagination, as they are for Cather. Cather shares all of the aforementioned traits with Southern writers, but it is her use of pastoral modes, more than any other fictional characteristic, that most reflects her Southern heritage and unites her work with the Southern literary imagination. The stages through which her variations on the pastoral advance correspond to a paradigm unique to Southern literature: the need to reclaim the pastoral ideal, followed by disillusionment and alienation, leading to a deep desire to reconcile human experience within a historical context.[10] Moreover, Cather also uses variations of the pastoral that duplicate those frequently found in Southern fiction. According to Lucinda MacKethan, "southern literature frequently takes as its departure point three specifically pastoral motifs: the urge to celebrate the simplicities of a natural order; the urge to idealize a golden age almost always associated with childhood; and the urge to criticize a contemporary social situation according to an earlier and purer set of standards."[11] Willa Cather, at various times, incorporates all of these Southern pastoral motifs into her work. Similarly, the themes surrounding her versions of the pastoral, particularly her treatment of exile and alienation, are also a product of her inherent Southern sensibility. For Cather, exile and alienation have their direct correlation in the postbellum experience of occupation, Reconstruction, and the westward migration of disillusioned Southerners.

While it may be true that "neither the antebellum South, of which her grandparents and parents often spoke, nor the South in reconstruc-

tion which she had known as a child became a temple of her imagination," [12] in any manifest sense, Cather's work is nonetheless replete with
allusions and images connected to these early years. Her Southern sen-
tience permeates what Jo Ann Middleton calls the "vacuoles" [13] of her
fiction. Through her use of pastoral modes, her Southern sensibility
emerges as yet another "thing not named": [14] the quiet center of Cather's
unspoken political views, a vision frequently elitist and often Old World
in its hierarchical dimensions.

The word "pastoral," for most readers, conjures up images of rural
life, of simpler times, of order and innocence. In the case of Southern
writers the pastoral plot was almost always one of domination by the
white patriarchy. Elizabeth Harrison argues convincingly, for example,
that the Southern pastoral version of the New Eden (what Louis Simpson
calls "the garden of the chattel" [15]) "served only the Southern white patriarchy," [16] which had designed a culture that associated women and
slaves with land ownership. The survival of the Southern agrarian system, and by extension, the Southern economy, depended on the myth
of an edenic plantation culture. For this reason, as Lucinda MacKethan
points out, the South has been the only region in America to identify
itself ideologically with the pastoral myth of Arcady. [17]

Simpson finds two distinct variations in the myth of this New World
pastoral: "a New England 'garden of the covenant' and," as previously
mentioned, "a Southern 'garden of the chattel.' " [18] While the early Virginians had originally established a covenant with God, as did their New
England counterparts, the covenant failed because their focus shifted to
commerce, particularly to the profits gleaned from raising tobacco. [19]
With the introduction of white bondmen, and later black slaves, to work
the fields, the Virginia plantation owners prospered and grew wealthy.
While seemingly feudal in structure, the widespread and systematic use
of African slave labor in the Southern states—although not entirely confined to the American South—conflicted with the democratic spirit.
Consequently, by the early eighteenth century, chattel slavery "de-
manded to be incorporated in the myth of the South" and its vision of
the edenic garden, [20] leaving the Southern literary imagination to find a
way to justify the presence of slavery in the redemptive garden.

The antebellum novels of William Gilmore Simms, John Pendleton
Kennedy, Nathaniel Beverly Tucker, and William Wirt, among others,

became the means by which the myth of harmonious plantation life was reinforced. W. J. Cash, Louis Simpson, and others have suggested this early pastoral tradition in Southern literature arose, out of necessity, as a means of defending chattel slavery. However, as Simpson points out, Southern literary minds, in attempting "to accommodate the pastoral mode to the antipastoral novelty of the South as expressed by the institution of African chattel slavery," ultimately produced what he terms a "culture of alienation."[21] Inevitably, these antebellum Southern writers found themselves cut off from the rest of the literary world by their connection to and acceptance of the politics of slavery.[22]

Although the Civil War abolished chattel slavery, it also destroyed the South's agrarian economic system. Without slave labor, landowners had no recourse but to hire workers to tend their fields. But the war had left many of them without the financial resources to do so. As Raymond Williams points out, the consequence of man's fall from grace was that he no longer could easily pick the fruits of nature but was condemned "to earn his bread in [sic] the sweat of his brow; that he had incurred, as his common fate, the curse of labour."[23] For the first time since the introduction of chattel slavery into the South, plantation owners had to earn their living without relying on the sweat of other brows.

While the plantation pastoral may have begun with the antebellum writers, the conditions imposed by Reconstruction gave rise to a new variation on the old myths, a unique version of Arcadia that continues, even today, as a major literary motif.[24] Postbellum writers began to envision a new Arcady, a vision of the antebellum plantation culture that evoked a nostalgic longing for the old ways.[25] Moreover, the Civil War, as Merrill Maguire Skaggs notes, "focused the nation's attention on the South," creating an interest in and a demand for Southern literature in both the North and the South.[26]

Wanting to present their region in the best light, the postwar South "found its literary outlet . . . in a lament for a lost Eden. . . . Literature was the last battleground on which the values of the Old South were tested."[27] The pastoral themes of exile and loss suited the ideological purpose of the postbellum writers. Thus they were strongly influenced, as was Willa Cather, by Virgil's *Eclogues* and the idylls of Theocritus. They identified with Virgil's visions of civil discord, occupation, and the expropriation of personal property, confirming Raymond Williams's contention that "the contrast within Virgilian pastoral is between the pleasures of rural settlement and the threat of loss or eviction."[28] Faced with postwar occupation, Southerners withdrew into their collective experience, an experience not only unique in the history of America but confined to a single region.[29]

As the rest of America put its postwar energy into creating new and better industries, the South continued to lag behind in production. To counterbalance the activity of the teeming North, Southern writers of the Reconstruction period envisioned a new Arcady. They created regional landscapes, visions of bucolic tranquility and simplicity, as a literary antidote to the thriving industrialization of the North and the migration of many of their discouraged countrymen to the wild and untamed West.

Postbellum writers Joel Chandler Harris (creator of the Uncle Remus stories among others), John Esten Cooke, Thomas Nelson Page, and others resurrected the myth of the edenic plantation, redeeming it from pre–Civil War Abolitionist fiction like Harriet Beecher Stowe's *Uncle Tom's Cabin*. By evoking romanticized images of the past and permeating them with a sense of loss and nostalgia, these writers created a vision of an ideal civilization, one threatened, like ancient Rome and Greece, with extinction. They frequently employed a common literary device: a loyal Negro narrating the plantation legends, bemoaning the loss of happier times, despite the abolition of slavery.[30] In this revised version of the pastoral plantation myth, the freed slave chooses to stay on and help his now "dependent" master. The irony, of course, although it eluded these early postbellum writers, was that the plantation economy and the welfare of the master and mistress had always been dependent on chattel slavery, an irony that would not escape Cather (as is evident in *Sapphira and the Slave Girl*) and subsequent Southern writers like Faulkner or Welty. As Francis Pendleton Gaines has pointed out, however, from a contemporary viewpoint, the faithful Negro narrator served as a literary device that intentionally presented "a beautiful felicity of racial contact," thus advancing a distorted view of race relations.[31] Willa Cather's family was very much a part of both the antebellum and postbellum Southern culture. Their presuppositions regarding relationships between blacks and whites, which would have included a belief in segregation, conformed to those of their fellow Southerners.

During her literary apprenticeship, Cather wrote two early short stories, "A Night at Greenway Court," and "The Elopement of Allen Poole" (published anonymously), using the South as her setting. A third story, "The Sentimentality of William Tavener," although not set in the South, nonetheless has Southern characters who, like her own family, have been transplanted to the West. Following these early experiments, Cather would not return to the South as her subject until her final novel *Sapphira and the Slave Girl*.[32]

Nevertheless, Cather's journey back to her ancestral roots through her fiction parallels the stages of the Southern literary experience: the need to find order in the pastoral ideal, the disillusionment that accompanies the inability to justify the historical reality with the mythical creation, followed by a strong desire to understand the past, no matter how painful, and the part it plays in the ongoing human drama.

# 1

## Cather's Southern Heritage and Pastoral Origins

VIRGINIA,
Earth's onely Paradise.

> . . . To whose, the golden Age
> Still Natures lawes doth give,
> —Michael Drayton
> "To the Virginian Voyage"

> I from my fatherland,
> My fatherland and pastures ever dear,
> To exile fly, . . .
> —Virgil, *Eclogues*

n her 1897 article on Frances Hodgson Burnett's *A Lady of Quality*, Willa Cather wrote that she did not believe we could "ever really outlive our past" that it "becomes a part of us, it is in our blood" (*WP* 359). Almost thirty years later her fictional creation Myra Henshawe seems to confirm those earlier sentiments when she tells Nellie Birdseye, "as we grow old we become more and more the stuff our forebears put into us. . . . We think we are so individual and so misunderstood when we are young; but the nature our strain of blood carries is inside there, waiting, like our skeleton" (*MME* 82). To understand the "nature" of Willa Cather's own "strain of blood," and how that consanguinity relates to her use of pastoral modes, we must look to her Southern roots.[1] Cather's consistent use of the pastoral which, as David Stouck notes, "informs to some degree almost all of her fiction," grew out of her need to ground her art in personal memory.[2]

For all her alleged detachment from her early roots, a close analysis of Cather's works yields a surprising wealth of themes and literary modes connecting her to the Southern literary tradition. In *The Roots of Southern Writing*, C. Hugh Holman contends that "at the heart of the Southern riddle [is] a union of opposites, a condition of instability, a paradox. Calm grace and raw hatred. Polished manners and violence. An intense individualism and intense group pressure toward conformity. A reverence to the point of idolatry of self-determining action and a caste and class structure presupposing an aristocratic hierarchy."[3] Almost any part of Holman's statement might be applied to Cather's work. Merrill Maguire Skaggs notes that Cather "almost compulsively created reversals in every element of the composition"[4] and that she often juxtaposed opposites. Exploring opposites in her fiction was perhaps Cather's method of evaluating, as well as giving equal credence to, both sides of an issue in an effort to unify the opposites into a personal wholeness. Hermione Lee also acknowledges Cather's doubleness, depicting her as both "a democrat and an élitist" often "pulled between the natural and the artificial, the native and the European," the "religious and fatalistic" and "equally interested in renunciation and possessiveness, in impersonality and obsession."[5] As if to confirm Holman's observation, Lee contends that "above all, there is a paradox for Cather in the act of writing itself."[6] While the condition of instability and the uniting of opposites is certainly not the exclusive territory of Southern writers, at the risk of simplifying a highly complex paradigm in Cather's fiction, I would suggest the impetus both to explore and to wed these opposing forces in her life does have its roots in her Southern heritage, most specifically in her family history, a family which embodied both Confederate and Union political sympathies during, and after, the Civil War.

Born in her grandmother Boak's home in Back Creek, Virginia, eight years after the end of the Civil War, Willa Cather spent the first nine years of her life in relative security and comfort. A year after her birth, she moved with her parents Charles and Mary Virginia Cather to the nearby Cather homestead, Willow Shade. Nestled in the Shenandoah Valley, with a splendid view of the Blue Ridge Mountains, the 331-acre Cather homestead[7] gave young Willa her first glimpse of what in retrospect must have seemed the idyllic pastoral setting. Built by her grandfather William Cather in 1851, Willow Shade was an impressive three-story brick home in the Greek Revival style popular at the time. A stately portico graced the front of the house, while four large surrounding willow trees afforded shade on hot summer days.[8]

Willa Cather's American heritage can be traced back to Jasper Cather, who emigrated from Northern Ireland to Pennsylvania in pre-revolutionary war years, and later to northwest Virginia. Cather was later informed by a distant cousin in England of a mutual relative who, in the seventeenth century, fought for Charles I and was subsequently given lands in Ireland by Charles II. According to James Woodress, a Cather coat of arms, sporting "a buck's head cabossed on a shield surmounted by a crest of a swan among reeds" and bearing "the motto 'Vigilans non cadet' ('He who is vigilant will not fall')"[9]—a motto which undoubtedly impressed Cather—is registered in British records of heraldry. Armed with her own proud lineage, Cather was not surprisingly drawn to those of aristocratic heritage.

As Hermione Lee and others have noted, Cather could be both democratic and elitist, as Southerners have traditionally been. She was often drawn to aristocratic personalities with artistic sensibilities, as is evident in her relationship with Stephen Tennant. But she was equally drawn to artists who had no aristocratic background, as her close devotion to Yehudi Menuhin during her later years indicates. She could befriend the immigrants of the Nebraska plains and ignore, as Elizabeth Shepley Sergeant tells us, the plight of the immigrants a few blocks from her New York apartment.[10] Cather's interest in and attraction to people of all classes, it seems, was based on individual relationships and situations. She could find the noble and heroic in the immigrant pioneer (Anna Pavelka, the prototype for Ántonia Shimerda), and conversely treat those with aristocratic pretensions, such as her protagonist Myra Henshawe, at times, unsympathetically. Nevertheless, Cather was acutely conscious of class distinctions, an awareness that most likely evolved from her childhood relationship with household servants (both black and white) in Virginia.

By the time Willa Cather was born, slavery had been abolished. But the families of both her parents, whether or not they condoned chattel slavery, were part of a culture whose economic stability had been based on the slave system. Rachel Seibert Boak, Cather's grandmother, who is the prototype for Rachel Blake in *Sapphira and the Slave Girl*, may have disapproved of slavery but like the rest of her family she supported the Confederacy and her three sons who fought in the war.[11] William Cather and his family, however, sympathized with the Union. Yet they were not averse to offering medical assistance to Confederate soldiers or turning their home into an emergency hospital when a measles epidemic threatened the Confederate troops.[12] The Cathers were first and foremost Southerners, and the compassion they showed in this crisis suggests an openness to judging circumstances on an individual basis, a trait Willa Cather seems to have inherited.

Many of the family members, like William Cather, were landowners and held political offices. Though middle class, they were a part of the antebellum society, as evidenced in their adherence to Southern customs and manners,[13] and likewise manifested through their class consciousness—social attitudes that would later influence Cather. Edith Lewis relates the story of one of Cather's favorite childhood games, a pastime that suggests the young Cather was already aware of her social position. Influenced by the stories her grandmother Boak read to her from Peter Parley's *Universal History*, she would make her own chariot by putting one chair upside down on top of another, then pretend to ride for hours imagining an "invisible slave" running beside her as he/she shouted, "Cato, thou art but man."[14] Moreover, according to family records, Rachel Seibert Boak's brother Henry Seibert, who had married a wealthy woman and kept slaves,[15] operated the Seibert Mill after 1856. Cather would later take the Seibert family name (spelling it Sibert) as her middle name. Although her intention was presumably to create a bond with her maternal grandmother, the name also links her with family members who were slave owners, an issue she confronts in *Sapphira*.

Although the William Cather family did not own slaves, they did have servants. An 1860 census shows two domestic workers listed as servants at Willow Shade: Abraham McDonald, age thirty-seven (mulatto), and Robert Leather, age eighteen (mulatto). While McDonald and Leather are listed as free, they may have been bound to William Cather for several years to learn tanning. An 1870 census lists two different servants, Eliza Page and George Washington, also black. Frederick County, unlike the eastern and southern areas of Virginia, had a large population of free blacks, but their status was far below that of the white population during that time.[16] These servants and those from the poor white families in the nearby mountains—including Mary Ann Anderson, her daughter Marjorie, and son Enoch, all of whom occasionally worked for the Cathers—were most likely paid with room and board and small gifts. During all her years as a domestic housekeeper in Nebraska for the Charles Cather family, Marjorie Anderson never received actual wages, though she had her own sleeping space and was treated as one of the family.[17]

Cather's early life in Virginia, as Edith Lewis recalls, "was one of great richness, tranquil and ordered and serene."[18] But there was also a dark side, the legacy of the Civil War and Reconstruction. Just as the country had been divided, so were Cather's paternal and maternal grandparents, taking opposite sides during the war. The very schism that ripped through the nation and later healed, leaving a scar, would do the same within her own family. Before the war ended, Cather's maternal grandparents William Lee Boak and Rachel Seibert Boak would lose one of their sons in the war. By contrast, Cather's paternal grandparents, William Cather and Caroline Smith Cather, Union sympathizers, would send their two sons, Cather's father Charles and his brother George, to West Virginia to wait out the war.

Because William Cather was a Union sympathizer, he suffered few losses during the war. His home (Willow Shade), land, and financial status remained relatively unaltered. But the families in the surrounding countryside were less fortunate. Struggling under the heavy yoke of Reconstruction, they resented the prosperity of William Cather and his family. He was ostracized by family and community members because of his Union ties[19] and because he and his two sons were awarded positions of authority by the military government. As sheriff of Frederick County, with the assistance of his sons Charles and George as deputies, William Cather continued to prosper in the Shenandoah Valley despite the tension with his relatives and neighbors.

Following her marriage to Charles, Mary Virginia Boak Cather attempted a reconciliation between William Cather and his relatives. A charming yet forceful woman, Virginia Cather paid each relative a personal visit to deliver an invitation to a Christmas party she had planned. Because the Boaks had been strong supporters of the Confederacy, and because the war had ended almost a decade before, the relatives acquiesced.

Once most of the family's scars had been healed, life at Willow Shade settled into its quiet rural existence. As Cather's close friend Dorothy Canfield Fisher once observed, Willa Cather lived her formative years "in a state which had the tradition of continuity and stability . . . and in a class which more than any other is always stubbornly devoted to the old ways of doing things."[20] That Cather spent part of her youth rebelling against "the old ways of doing things" is a well-established fact. What is important, however, is her return to the established Old World cultural values of her youth in her middle and later years.[21]

Although Cather may not have written overtly about the South,[22] many of her Virginia childhood experiences would later inform her fiction. Edith Lewis tells the story of young Cather's delight in quilting with the old women in the region,[23] an event that would later evolve into the numerous quilting, sewing, and tailoring metaphors Cather used in her fiction. In a letter to Mrs. Ackroyd, Cather tells how Mary Ann Anderson's stories about the locals delighted her during Cather's 1896 visit to Virginia. (Anderson is the prototype for Mrs. Ringer in *Sapphira*.)[24] This oral story-telling tradition is evident in Cather's narrative technique of inserting stories within stories. Mildred Bennett also acknowledges Cather's Virginia years as influential in affording her an "introduction to nature . . . American history, and the Old World."[25] Charles Cather shared his passionate love of history (particularly history associated with his local heritage) with his daughter, often calling on the young Willa to discourse on life in Virginia in the Miner Brothers' General Store in Red Cloud.[26] His knowledge of history was yet another strong influence on Cather, evident in her historical fiction, especially in *Sapphira*, which makes abundant use of the historical details from family history and her Virginia childhood. But Charles Cather influenced her in other ways as well. For it is the image of her father as a shepherd in the pastoral Shenandoah Valley that would capture Willa Cather's childhood imagination, an image that would remain with her for her entire life.[27]

On the one hand Charles Cather was a gentleman farmer, a man of refinement and courteous manners, but he also raised sheep for the Baltimore market. The image of Cather's father as a shepherd in a bucolic[28] landscape is evoked in the pastoral poem, "The Swedish Mother," which Cather included in the 1923 edition of *April Twilights and Other Poems*.

A Swedish mother recounts the story of her own early childhood to her young daughter, " 'way back in old countree,' " when her father brought the sheep home from the field " 'way up on hill, / Ten times high like our windmill' " (52) on a spring evening. Critics generally agree the poem reflects one of Cather's earliest memories. The Swedish mother may have been thinking of her beloved homeland across the sea, but Cather's "old countree," with its mountains and sheep, is northwest Virginia, where she had spent much of her time in the fields with her father, helping to herd the sheep.

Cather's father obviously influenced her pastoral vision, but her mother also helped to shape Cather's literary imagination. Edith Lewis describes Virginia Cather as "a handsome, imperious woman, with a strong will . . . full of quick, eager impulses—quick to resent, quick to sympathize, headstrong, passionate, and yet capable of great kindness and understanding."[29] Although she was a stern disciplinarian, she nevertheless allowed her children the freedom and individuality to do as they pleased except where household rules applied. Virginia Cather was a product of her genteel Southern upbringing, obsessed with "the proper way of doing things."[30] Cather would later adopt her mother's "benevolent, if distant, desire to champion the underprivileged or misunderstood."[31] The influence of her mother's teaching was evident even in Cather's early years, when she opened her tin bank and gave all of her money to Uncle Billy Parks, a poor broom-maker who was lodged for the night at Willow Shade.[32] Thus the tradition of noblesse oblige was very much a part of Cather's Southern upbringing, eventually evolving into a class awareness that would permeate much of her fiction. Years later, Cather would create a fairly accurate portrait of Virginia Cather in the character of Mrs. Templeton, in the semi-autobiographical story "Old Mrs. Harris." Mrs. Templeton, a genteel Southern lady, discreetly provides "the poor Maude children," whose mother is the Templeton's laundress, with dimes to purchase ice cream at the church supper, and then seats them at a table with her own children (OD 122–23).

Willa Cather's complex, ambiguous, and often difficult relationship with her mother has been admirably and thoroughly explored by Sharon O'Brien in Willa Cather: The Emerging Voice. As O'Brien, Lewis, and others have noted, the aristocratic women[33] of Cather's later works bear remarkable similarities to the charming, haughty, imperious Virginia

Cather. We see her in the energetic, vivacious, and flirtatious Marian Forrester, in the tormented and exiled figure of Myra Henshawe, and in the
strong, matriarchal antebellum personality of Sapphira Colbert who,
like Virginia Cather, allowed no one to see her until her hair had been
pinned up and she was perfectly groomed.[34] Bernice Slote suggests that
Willa Cather was motivated by three often incompatible drives: "to win
out with a career, to be a success in a world of mostly men, . . . to be the
artist, as great an artist as she might be; . . . and . . . to be a Virginia lady,
like her mother."[35] This third drive appears to conflict with Edith Lewis's
oft-quoted statement that as a child Cather felt stifled by "the polite,
rigid social conventions of that Southern society. . . . If one fell in with
those sentimental attitudes, those euphuisms that went with good manners," Lewis tells us, "one lost all touch with reality, with truth of experience."[36] But Cather's need to separate herself from her mother was
more than a rejection of social conventions. She also needed to understand their relationship, an understanding that would eventually lead to
her recognition and acceptance of their likeness.[37]

This mode of separation took the form of a rebellion against not
only her mother but also her mother's gender. For at age fourteen, four
years after her family's move to Nebraska, Willa Cather emerged as the
rebellious "William Cather, Jr.," hair cropped boyishly short, dressed in
mannish clothes, brazenly flaunting the conventions of the day. But her
behavior was more than a rebellion against her mother and Southern traditions. It was also linked to being unwillingly uprooted from her Virginia home and transported to the barren plains of Nebraska.[38]

The pressures of Reconstruction and the desire to begin anew were
the impetus for the migration West of many Southerners. By 1882, all of
the William Cather family had migrated to the plains of Nebraska, with
the exception of his son Charles's family. Only after the devastating loss
of their sheep barn in a fire did Willa Cather's father decide to join his
brother and parents in the Midwest. By then, his own family had grown
to six, including Willa, her two younger brothers Roscoe and Douglass,
and her younger sister Jessica.[39]

"In a deep sense, the mission of America has been to make all things
new," wrote Robert Penn Warren. "This continent was a new Eden in
which man would miraculously assume his prelapsarian condition, and
the movement westward was a perpetual baptism into a new inno-

cence."[40] Thus, in their move westward, Willa Cather's family was reenacting the American pastoral myth, a myth that portrays America as the new Garden of Eden[41] where man is offered a second chance to change the course of history. If Willa Cather had been exiled from her Southern Garden of Eden, just as Virgil's Meliboeus is exiled from Arcadia, she and her family were nevertheless offered a fresh start in the wilderness of Nebraska. It was an experience that would imprint itself on her impressionable young mind and would later emerge in the Virgilian themes of loss and eviction—specifically her fictional treatment of exile and homesickness—within her pastoral vision. Nevertheless, the transition to this new world was extremely traumatic for Cather.

Edith Lewis tells us Cather loved "passionately . . . every tree and rock, every landmark of the countryside, all the familiar faces, all their 'things' at Willowshade, all their ways,"[42] despite her rebellion against Southern customs and manners.[43] But whatever her love/hate relationship with Southern social conventions, the move, at such an impressionable age, was particularly difficult for Willa Cather. One of her last memories of Virginia was watching their beloved sheepdog Old Vic, who had broken loose from her new home with a neighbor, come running toward them, dragging her chain, as they were boarding the train—a vivid, poignant experience that all but broke Cather's heart.[44] But what lay ahead was perhaps the most painful shock of all. As Cather once told a colleague at *McClure's Magazine,* "The move at such a tender age from the damp, shady, mountainous beauty of the Shenandoah Valley to a raw, treeless and nearly waterless land had been cruel for a child."[45]

In the years following her success, Cather often spoke in interviews of the pain and confusion of being uprooted from her Virginia home. Speaking of her introduction to the Nebraska plains in a 1913 interview in the *Philadelphia Record* Cather confessed: "I would not know how much a child's life is bound up in the woods and hills and meadows around it, if I had not been jerked away from all these and thrown out into a country as bare as a piece of sheet iron" (*KA* 448). Describing her family's trip into the barren country, as she rode on "hay in the bottom of a Studebaker wagon," Cather remarked that she "felt a good deal as if we had come to the end of everything—it was a kind of erasure of personality" (448).

Five years later, in her fourth novel *My Ántonia,* these strong senti-

ments are expressed by her character Jim Burden who, like Cather, is
taken from his Virginia home and put on a train bound for Nebraska.
The passage reveals much of Cather's own pain, homesickness, and loneliness during her exile from the bucolic, serene Shenandoah Valley to the
barren wilderness of the Nebraska Divide. Peering over the edge of the
hay wagon, as had the young Willa Cather, Jim Burden reflects: "I had
the feeling that the world was left behind, that we had got over the edge
of it, and were outside man's jurisdiction. I had never before looked up
at the sky when there was not a familiar mountain ridge against it. . . .
Between that earth and that sky I felt erased, blotted out" (8). Although
Jim Burden claims not to be homesick, he is acutely aware of the homesickness of others and seems to intuit that Mr. Shimerda's suicide was
the result of his displacement (66). He is equally aware of Lena's homesickness when she is living in town (111), as well as Ántonia's when she
tells him of her old town where her grandmother lived. "My feet remember all the little paths through the woods" (151), she tells Jim, echoing
Cather's similar comment on her first return trip to Gore, Virginia: "I
went down a road and found I knew what was coming next all the way
along" (WCP 136). In fact, both Cather and her mother were extremely
homesick their first year on the plains. As Cather remarked in a 1921 interview, "I was little and homesick and lonely and my mother was homesick and nobody paid any attention to us" (WCP 32). Suffering with
stomach contractions brought on by homesickness, young Cather made
a pact with herself. She "would not eat much until [she] got back to Virginia and could get some fresh mutton" (KA 448).

Cather's first return trip to Virginia in 1896 was filled with pleasant
memories. She bicycled through the Shenandoah Valley,[46] and she
walked up the Hollow Road to visit Mary Ann Anderson who had cared
for her when she was ill as a child and who at that time shared her memorable repertoire of stories with her.[47] Family photographs show her at the
creek near Rockman Road, on the Hollow Road, in the Arboretum, on
the steps at "Auntie Gore's," and happily discovering the old rabbit traps
where she had left them in the woods thirteen years earlier.[48]

Her delight in coming East after thirteen years in Nebraska was evident even before her trip to Gore. For as soon as her train was east of
Chicago, where she could see trees, hills, and clean streams, she realized
she didn't need a mint julep to know she was returning to her roots. Even

the conductor noted her expression of delight, asking her if she was coming back home.[49]

The 9 August 1913 *Philadelphia Record* interview, mentioned earlier,
took place before Cather's return in September to Gore (Back Creek),
Virginia, for her second visit. But this time her trip to Virginia was a
disappointment. As letters to Elizabeth Shepley Sergeant reveal, Cather
made the best of what was obviously a painful experience. Many of the
people she knew and loved had died,[50] as had her great-aunt Sidney Gore.
She found the town dull, was unimpressed by the food, and discovered
she "no longer cared about the holy and sacred peculiarities of the people
she knew when she was little."[51] She expressed her disappointment over
finding the place "dismal, ghostly and a bit sentimental," but after beginning a routine of daily six-mile walks in the rain with her companion
Isabelle McClung, she was refreshed by all the natural, untamed beauty.[52]

To the nine-year-old Cather, uprooted from her Virginia home, the
natural, untamed beauty on the Divide had proved to be something quite
different: no valleys with fields, or pine woods, or laurel, or acacia trees,
nothing but miles of prairie grass and an occasional lone cottonwood.
The large imposing brick structure of Willow Shade was replaced by a
cramped story-and-a-half home in Red Cloud where young Cather must
have resented sharing an attic room, crowded with three double beds in
barracks formation, with her brothers and sisters.[53] Not until her mid-
twenties, while living in Pittsburgh in the solid comfortable home of the
McClungs, who, like the Cathers of Willow Shade, employed well-
trained servants, would she once again find the orderly routine of her
former Virginia home.[54]

Although the Southern umbilical cord had been severed, Cather's
Southern heritage was in her blood; it traveled with her in the form of
her family and their few possessions. Her mother insisted on bringing
the Confederate flag and the sword that had belonged to her brother
William who had died in the war. Moreover, the Cathers' belongings
were packed in crates and boxes using Confederate money as packing
material, rather than old newspapers. Four years later, when Willa and
the neighborhood children created their town, Sandy Point (constructed
of the packing boxes), they used this same Confederate money as their
currency.

Two other members of the Cather household joined them on their

journey West: the housekeeper Marjorie Anderson (Mary Ann Anderson's daughter) and her brother Enoch. Marjorie's favorite pastime was
talking about Virginia and the people back home, and Charles Cather
kept Marjorie apprised of all the news from Winchester in the weekly
paper to which he subscribed.[55] Years after Cather had left Nebraska, her
return visits home would include long talks with Marjorie on the back
porch or in the sunny kitchen.[56] In many ways, Marjorie, like Cather's
mother and Grandmother Boak, kept Virginia alive for the rest of them.

In fact a small Virginian community had already taken root on the
Nebraska plains in the form of "New Virginia," a settlement not far from
Catherton, where Willa Cather's Uncle George and Aunt Franc and other
Virginians from the Winchester area resided. Like Cather's grandfather,
father, and her Uncle George, these families envisioned a land of new
promise. Moreover, these transplanted Southerners brought with them
all the old values: "individualism, localism, family, clan, and rural folk
culture."[57] Cather later described these fellow Southerners as a clannish
set (a term she also used to describe the immigrant groups) but acknowledged their cultural side, explaining that although they had the usual
country "Literary" it was on a better scale than most.[58]

Through the semi-autobiographical story "Old Mrs. Harris," we
learn a great deal about the lifestyle and attitudes of the Templeton
(Cather) family. The narrator twice refers to their servant Mandy (modeled after Marjorie Anderson) as "the bound girl." Mr. Templeton (modeled after Charles Cather) tells the children Uncle Remus stories (Joel
Chandler Harris's classic expressions of the postbellum plantation pastoral) after dinner. The character of Grandmother Harris, based on
Rachel Boak, has assumed the role of housekeeper, the only household
position acceptable for a widowed mother-in-law, a role that "back in
Tennessee . . . was not exceptional, but perfectly regular" (OD 129-30). In
the South, "when a woman was a widow and had married daughters, she
considered herself an old woman and wore full-gathered black dresses
and a black bonnet and became a housekeeper" (132).

"Mrs. Harris and her 'things,' " we are told, "were almost required to
be invisible" (OD 98). She often thinks of the old days back home in
Tennessee (Virginia), regretting the garden and the apple trees she had
to leave behind, calling to mind once again images of exile from the Garden of Eden. Yet the narrator tells us that Mrs. Harris no longer lived "in

a feudal society, where there were plenty of landless people glad to render service to the more fortunate" (133). Ironically, Mandy "the bound girl" is seemingly discounted in this statement.

Because of these surrounding influences from her "old countree," the young Willa formed a close bond with the immigrants on the plains. She loved their stories and could fully empathize with their homesickness. If no one in her grandfather's house, except her mother, could understand what this traumatic uprooting had meant to her, then surely these people from across the ocean, who had left their homeland, extended families, and most of their possessions behind, would sympathize with her plight. Thus Willa Cather and the immigrant pioneer women of the plains shared a common bond through their loneliness. Cather's allusions to *Robinson Crusoe* and *The Swiss Family Robinson* in all of her plains novels further suggest she perceived prairie life as being shipwrecked on an island, cut off from the civilized world. Both books convey a sense of isolation and loneliness that seem to reflect Cather's own confused feelings about her Nebraska childhood.

All about her, Cather saw the immigrants struggle to preserve their own culture within a new one, holding on to old values while adopting new ones in order to survive in the New World. She, too, must have felt the need to assimilate, although the "old values" would still remain very much a part of her daily home life. C. Vann Woodward contends that it is not uncommon for a Southerner, once outside his territory, to "yield to the impulse to suppress the identifying idiom, to avoid the awkward subject, and to blend inconspicuously into the national pattern—to act the role of the standard American."[59] For Willa Cather, the desire to "suppress the identifying idiom" came when she was enrolled in the Red Cloud school. Aware that her speech was different from that of her classmates, she worked to eliminate her Southern accent.[60] According to James Woodress, however, Cather retained vestiges of her Southern mode of speech and was taken by surprise, while on vacation in New England in 1942, by a man who said he recognized her by her Southern accent.[61]

Her family also retained their Southern ways, sitting "about in leisurely conversation," rarely in a hurry to tend to the business or problems at hand.[62] Cather, however, rejected her family's easygoing Southern attitudes. Ambitious and filled with plans for the future, she read voluminously, studied Latin and Greek with a local scholar, and plotted her course for the University of Nebraska, her first step in her flight from a place she sometimes referred to as Siberia.[63] Yet, curiously, when she chose her fictional settings, it was the Nebraska wilderness rather than the lush Shenandoah Valley that stirred her imagination during most of her writing career.

Several of Cather's biographers have acknowledged her reticence to use her Southern background. Edith Lewis alludes to Cather's reluctance to write about the South as "some sort of inhibition" that kept her from using the wealth of stories and events from her Southern past, but she offers no explanation for this reticence.[64] James Woodress suggests that Cather's "mixed emotions" about Virginia and her Southern heritage were a deterrent to writing about her early experiences.[65] Virginia Verle (Lady Falls) Brown concludes Cather's reluctance to write about the South evolved from her "ambivalent feelings about her parents, who epitomized for her the best and the worst of the Southern genteel tradition."[66] Although all of these are viable explanations for Cather's dismissal of her Southern material, I would like to suggest another possibility, which is in some ways an extension of Woodress's perception: At the heart of Cather's "mixed emotions" toward her Southern heritage is an inability to reconcile her childhood pastoral vision of the South with her adult awareness of the post–Civil War Reconstruction reality.

At the imaginative core of the pastoral ideal is Cather's penchant for the heroic. She was drawn to the artistic aristocracy: musicians, writers, actors, and singers, whom she envisioned as heroic in their struggle for success. But her hero worship extended beyond an admiration for artists to the great military leaders of the ages: Napoleon, Caesar, and Alexander the Great, all of whom, particularly Napoleon, are mentioned numerous times in her early novels. Although France would later come to embody for her many of the Old World values that she felt modern industrial America lacked, Rome and Caesar also occupied her imagination. Rome, as she wrote to a friend, was the one place she most wanted to see.[67] Even in an early childhood scrapbook, apparently brought from Virginia, Cather wrote in her childish scrawl on the left side of a picture of a toga-clad cherubic figure, "I am a Roman citizen!"; on the right side of the picture, she signed her name: Willa.[68]

Her attraction to ancient civilizations like Rome is not surprising. Rome, like the antebellum South, had been a highly cultured civilization with a dark side that had known war and ultimately, defeat. The South, unlike the rest of the nation, shares a past, a heritage of defeat and human suffering that connects it to "the common lot of mankind" rather than to our "national legends of opulence and success and innocence."[69] Thus, like many Southerners, Cather felt at times a stronger connection to Europe than to America. This affinity is evident in her use of Rome as a metaphor for the demise of the Old South. In the 1923 edition of *April Twilights and Other Poems,* she published three poems about ancient Rome and Caesar: "The Palatine (in the 'Dark Ages')"—originally published in *McClure's* in 1909 and much admired by a fellow Southerner, Mark Twain[70]—"The Gaul in the Capitol," and "A Likeness (Portrait Bust of an Unknown, Capitol, Rome)." Although Cather deleted from this edition her poem "The Namesake," a tribute to her uncle William Seibert Boak who had fallen in battle during the Civil War,[71] she added the poems about Caesar and ancient Rome that symbolically connote the same theme and subject. "The Namesake" laments the early death of a Confederate soldier, acknowledges his family connections with the poet, and praises his courage and "proud blood." The poet, as if to make up for her relative's defeat, concludes the poem by metaphorically taking up the flag: "And I'll be winner at the game / Enough for two who bore the name." The same theme appears in the later poem, "The Palatine," suggesting Cather wrote it as an extended metaphor for the occupied South. In "The Palatine," an older brother shares the images of Rome's defeat with his younger brother. Caesar's home lies in ruins where goats and cattle wander about the marble chambers, now open to the sky. Poverty looms over the ancient palace: " 'The times are bad and the world is old— / Who knows the where of the Caesars' gold.' " Caesar's brave soldiers have met their doom, " 'Dogs in the kennel and wolf in the den / Howl for the fate of the Caesars' men. / Slain in Asia, slain in Gaul, / By Dacian border and Persian wall.' " Just as in "The Namesake," "Two by two and three by three / Missouri lies by Tennessee; / Row on row, an hundred deep, / Maryland and Georgia sleep; / Wistfully the poplars sigh / Where Virginia's thousands lie," Caesar's men also lie slain on battlefields. Both "The Gaul in the Capitol" and "A

Likeness" talk of the glories ("The Julians, gigantic in armour"), the defeat ("An empire, long in ashes lying"), and the weaknesses ("His look arraigns a social order / Somehow entrammelled with his pain") and ("Tricked by the forms of things material") of the Roman empire. "A Likeness" suggests yet another connection between Cather's Old South and Rome. The poem tells of a youth caught up in the transition and ultimate defeat of a cultured, yet corrupt, civilization. The title not only links the two youths—the boy in this poem with the boy in "The Namesake"—but also the two civilizations: ancient Rome and the antebellum South.

In 1907, while working at *McClure's*, Cather wrote a short story also entitled "The Namesake." But unlike the poem the story is set in Pennsylvania, and the young hero is a Union soldier whose memory is honored by the narrator, his nephew. Why Cather chose to camouflage her Southern roots in this story remains a mystery, particularly when her earlier identification with her Uncle William, who had died for the Confederacy, had been so strong. Perhaps, having begun a new life in the Northeast, she felt a need to conform or to establish an alternate identity. Woodward contends that "the same urge to conformity that operates upon ethnic or national minorities to persuade them to reject identification with their native heritage or that of their forebears operates to a degree upon the Southerner as well."[72] Still, autobiographical elements do inform "The Namesake." The narrator tells us that his father was considered a renegade because he did not return home to join the army and fight in the war, just as Charles Cather was sent to West Virginia (actually only five miles from Back Creek) by his father, and waited out the war in relative safety. Similarly, just as Cather's uncle William Seibert Boak was killed in the war, the fictive uncle (here half-brother to the narrator's father) also dies in battle. While she merges the experiences of both sides of her family, she nevertheless denies her uncle and her mother's side of the family (the Boaks) their Confederate allegiance. Hence, there is a certain irony when the narrator, at the end of the story, asserts, "For the first time I felt the pull of race and blood and kindred, and felt beating within me things that had not begun with me" (*CFS* 146). The conclusion of the story suggests Cather clung to the heroic dimensions she associated with her uncle and with battle, while seeming to eschew any connection with the South. Cather's earlier choice of the name William Cather, Jr., when she was fourteen, can be viewed as her way of uniting her patriarchal and matriarchal heritage, and of reuniting both North and South. By appropriating the first name of both her grandfathers, as well as her uncle "Who once bore a name like mine," Cather was making one of her many attempts to unify one of the opposing forces in her life.[73] But by 1923, when the second edition of *April Twilights* was published, Cather's ambivalent feelings about the South had been strengthened by her disappointing 1913 visit to her birthplace. All about her she had seen poverty and what she perceived as a "shiftlessness" in the Southern people she encountered. Against this harsh and demeaning reality, the image of the cultured civilization that had once been the Old South was difficult to sustain. Quite possibly Cather, who would "be winner at the game," chose not to identify with the postwar South.

Cather's association of ancient Rome with the Old South is further demonstrated by her passion for the works of Virgil and her appropriation of his pastoral motifs, which incorporate, according to Leo Marx, "a delicate blend of myth and reality" within a symbolic landscape.[74] Virgil's *Eclogues*, the first of which is sometimes referred to as "The Dispossessed," must have touched her deeply. Meliboeus, his home and land taken from him, forced into exile, laments his departure to the shepherd Tityrus, once a slave of Rome, who now happily resides in the countryside with his flock as a free man.

> In the wide-branching beech-trees' shade reclined
> Thou, Tityrus, playst on thy slender reed
> A shepherd song. I from my fatherland,
> My fatherland and pastures ever dear,
> To exile fly, while Tityrus at ease
> In cooling shadows bids the woodland sing
> Of lovely Amaryllis.[75]

This passage must have triggered young Cather's own painful memories of exile from the pastures of her "fatherland." The dispossession here is a politically motivated one, based on the action of the Roman government to expropriate the property of small landowners, Virgil's among them, for the purpose of rewarding military veterans—not unlike the expropriation of the property of many Southern landowners in the occupation after the Civil War. Thus *Eclogues* poignantly acknowledges "the implacable character of the forces threatening established order."[76] These Virgilian pastorals become the poet's quest for order, one that he will seek through his "discovery" of Arcady, in much the same way that Willa Cather will later employ pastoral modes in her own search for order and meaning.

> And will there be
> Some godless soldier on my well-tilled farm?
> Some grim barbarian, gathering its yield?
> Oh, to what woes has civil discord led
> Our wretched countrymen! For whom to reap
> Were these fair acres sown? What profit now
> My grafted pear-trees and my trellised vine?
> Move on, dear flock, whose happy days are done![77]

Many Southerners must have shared Meliboeus's sentiments as he ponders how "civil discord" has led to his exile. Cather, too, saw "happy days" taken from her when she was "exiled" from Willow Shade. Her expulsion from what must have seemed an idyllic world would later become the impetus for her employment of the pastoral mode in her work. Like many postbellum Southern writers, who found their arcadian world torn away from them after the war, Cather created a fictional retreat, her private Arcady. Her early short stories and poems are replete with sentimental pastoral visions. Only later, in her novels, would she begin to explore the ironic underside of the pastoral, paralleling the work of postbellum writers such as Ellen Glasgow and anticipating the writings of Faulkner and Welty.

In a 1925 article in *The New Republic,* Elizabeth Shepley Sergeant, writing about Cather, who was then in her fifties, claims, "She has told us nothing yet in fiction about Virginia and her early childhood, though she sometimes speaks of them, recalling her revolts from certain polite feudal traditions and stratifications which were borne away on a wild breeze when she reached the Divide."[78] Sergeant seems to suggest that an almost baptismal cleansing took place when Cather was removed from her "feudal traditions" and bathed in the "wild breeze" of the Divide.

But although it may appear on the surface that Cather's subjects and set-tings were primarily non-Southern, on closer inspection, we begin to re-alize that she has indeed told us much about Virginia and her childhood. Her Southern sensibility permeates all of her work, most often through her use of the pastoral.

# 2

# Cather's New World Pastorals

> Come my tan-faced children,
> Follow well in order, get your weapons ready,
> Have you your pistols? have you your sharp-edged
> axes?
>> Pioneers! O pioneers!
>>> —Whitman, "Pioneers, O Pioneers!"

Cather may have found the postbellum South a psychologically inappropriate subject for her heroic visions;[1] however, the West, with its myth of "virgin" territory and new beginnings for the stalwart and brave, suited her sensibility perfectly. The early pioneers and their struggles had heroic stature, whereas Southerners were still burdened with Reconstruction. Moreover, the new West was ideally suited to the pastoral mode. The West was the New World, a prelapsarian condition that afforded new beginnings. Not surprisingly, then, Cather's stories and early plains novels incorporate variations on this pastoral ideal. Her early short stories, written while she was still in college, were for the most part negative.[2] Testifying to the grim and harsh realities the immigrants faced on the plains, the stories exemplify Cather's pastoral themes of exile and loss. Her first published story "Peter" tells of the suicide of a dispossessed Bohemian musician living on the Divide with his large family and success-driven son. The grim details of the suicide would later appear in *My Ántonia*, suggesting the incident's strong emotional and psychological impact on Cather's imagination.[3] Her second published story "Lou, the Prophet" focuses on a Danish man driven to reli-

gious fanaticism by the isolation on the Divide. We are informed early in
these stories that both men miss their homeland. Peter is "very homesick
for Bohemia" (*CSF* 542). Lou has "been in the West for seven years, but
he had never quite gotten over his homesickness for Denmark" (535). Implicit in these stories is Cather's own inability to come to terms with her
lingering homesickness. She and the country may have "had it out together" (*WCP* 32) in her first year on the Divide, and perhaps "that
shaggy grass country" did indeed grip her "with a passion" she was never
"able to shake" (32). Nevertheless she chose to make her home in the
East, and her burial site, in the shadow of Mt. Monadnock, in New
Hampshire, is in an area not unlike her childhood home in Virginia.

Other early stories tell of the inhumane treatment of a Russian immigrant ("The Clemency of the Court") and a Norwegian driven to al-
coholism and desperate measures by isolation and loneliness ("On the
Divide"). David Stouck sees these early stories as pastorals not because
of their rural setting but because Cather is writing in the tradition of
Wordsworth, whose poems sometimes championed the poor and down-
trodden, and because "she identifies imaginatively with the humbleness
and loneliness" in the lives of these immigrants.[4] Cather, indeed, projects
her deep feelings of homesickness on these outcasts. But, like Wordsworth, she was also writing from a privileged position.[5] Ellen Moers tells
us Cather "was very well aware she herself came from 'old' people, that
is, good, solid, Eastern-seaboard Virginian stock. And the 'new' people
she encountered were crude, poor, not well spoken, servant people who
had illegitimate children and were dirty people."[6] Cather's subjects are
not so much evidence of her support for the lower classes (although she
did care deeply about those who had become her friends) as they are pro-
jections of her own emotional state.

Only after Willa Cather moved from Nebraska to Pittsburgh in 1896
do we begin to see subtle changes in her sentiments toward the plains
and a variation from her use of the Virgilian pastoral themes of exile and
loss to an idealization of a time associated with childhood, a key pastoral
motif in Southern literature.[7] The 1902 story "The Treasure of Far Island" contains none of the negative features of the earlier fiction written
while Cather was still in Nebraska. On the contrary, the story is a nostalgic return to the treasured memories of her Nebraska childhood. The
setting, Empire City, is Cather's Red Cloud. In "Treasure," the main

character, successful playwright Douglass Burnham, returns to his hometown, renews his acquaintance with his childhood friend Margie, and together they return to the sandbar island along the Republican River (the same setting where Jim Burden will later spend a memorable afternoon with the hired immigrant girls in *My Ántonia*) to recover a jar containing the buried treasures of those earlier years spent together with their group of friends. But their "golden days" have long since "died in a blaze of glory" (*CSF* 281). Douglass confesses to Margie his deeper feelings from those earlier times, the moment in which he realized his love for her. In "that moment," he tells her, "we grew up, and shut the gates of Eden behind us" (281).

As late as 1909 Cather wrote yet another pastoral of childhood, "The Enchanted Bluff." Once again the setting is the Republican River. The young narrator, who is about to leave the area to teach in another district, acknowledges he is already homesick. Together with his five closest friends, he spends the night on their sandbar island while his friends revel in the possibilities and mysteries awaiting them. They tell stories of the Aztecs and the Spanish conquerors, of Coronado and his men, and of the Cliff Dwellers who lived and died on top of a large rock called the Enchanted Bluff. This latter story—one that anticipates the appearance of cliff-dweller stories in three of Cather's novels, *The Song of the Lark, The Professor's House,* and *Death Comes for the Archbishop*—captures the imaginations of the boys, who dream of one day scaling the side. As the narrator (twenty years later) reveals at the end of the story, however, his former childhood companions (now grown men) may continue to dream and talk of one day exploring the bluff, but they have long since settled into conventional lives that preclude any such achievement. Written seven years after "The Treasure of Far Island," "The Enchanted Bluff" signifies, as Hermione Lee has pointed out, yet another shift in Cather's use of the pastoral: the introduction of regret and failure,[8] themes that Cather will later weave into the pastoral tapestry of her novels.

*O Pioneers!* is the first of her novels to incorporate the Virgilian pastoral, with a focus on the themes of exile and loss.[9] As Sharon O'Brien points out, Cather's "concern with uprooting, transplanting, and resettlement"[10] informs much of her later work. Thus the plight of the immigrants was an apt subject for her second novel. But although Cather championed the immigrants, immortalizing their heroic struggles in print, she was still, for all her democratic efforts, acutely aware of class distinctions, a product of her Southern upbringing. At home and comfortable with the immigrants she considered her friends, Cather was usually more reserved around those from the working classes with whom she was not personally acquainted.[11]

Cather's need to mythologize the "peasants in the field," while simultaneously setting herself apart from them, is consistent with those who write in the pastoral tradition.[12] The pastoral plot for Southern writers, for example, was almost always one of domination by the white patriarchy.[13] Thus it is not surprising that Cather's New Eden reflects these elements of class consciousness.

Indeed, Cather's appropriation of the immigrant pioneer story served a twofold purpose. The first, as mentioned earlier, was a means of telling her own emotional story of displacement, homesickness, and adjustment through the experience of non-native-born Americans. The second was to espouse a capitalist agrarian system where farmers who worked hard could prosper and grow wealthy within their lifetimes.

The frontier, John Randall tells us, gave rise to the "natural aristocrat," the Carlylian dynamic of "heroes and ordinary people": those who are leaders and those who are led.[14] This New World of the Midwestern plains also held myriad possibilities for Jefferson's yeoman farmer. Paradoxically, Alexandra Bergson embodies both Jefferson's yeoman and Randall's "natural aristocrat." Initially, she is the yeoman farmer, signifying the repudiation of both the old European feudal systems and the Southern version of an Arcady based on the institution of slavery. She not only represents a "pastoral purification"[15] of the agrarian vision but, as Sharon O'Brien and others have noted, a re-visioning of the creation story.[16] Cather transforms the male pastoral tradition into "celebrations of female heroism."[17] Moreover, she also celebrates "the simplicities of a natural order" (another Southern pastoral motif)[18] through the character of Alexandra who, as O'Brien contends, "defines herself in relation to—instead of against—the natural world."[19]

Southern women writers, in particular, have always understood the connection between women, nature, and the land, eventually appropriating the male pastoral archetype and making it their own. They sought a new female protagonist, as Elizabeth Harrison points out, "beyond symbolic representation as virginal or despoiled land."[20] Harrison sees Cather's *O Pioneers!* as the first successful narrative to change the relationship between women and the land.[21] Thus it helped to pave the way for Southern women writers to re-vision the women's role in the pastoral myth which in the male Southern pastoral plot had always equated them with property.

In Cather's re-visioning of the creation story, Eve, once burdened with the responsibility for the fall of man as told in the male narrative, now redeems herself through establishing a New Eden. Alexandra, personifying Eve, reclaims the garden from the wilderness. Yet Alexandra, like her aristocratic counterparts in the antebellum South, never literally labors in the earth. Symbolically, she may fulfill her role in the reclamation of a New Eden, but a closer analysis of her position reveals a side more compatible with Cather's Southern sensibility, that of Randall's natural aristocrat.

Throughout *O Pioneers!* the goal of first John Bergson and then his daughter Alexandra is to reach that Golden Age, when the ripe, fertile land will continue to produce on its own, without human toil. For it is manual labor that distinguishes the common man from the gentleman. Alexandra's father tries to protect her from working in the fields, telling her brothers they should hire help. Moreover, we never actually see Alexandra physically exerting herself (although it is implied). Carl finds her "standing lost in thought" as she leans on her pitchfork in the garden (29), rather than digging for the sweet potatoes. Throughout the book, we see her in similar static poses, frequently dreaming or planning for the future when she and her brothers will be rich, independent landowners, and Emil will go to school. By Part Two, sixteen years later, her dream has been realized. Seated at the head of her table, she presides over her hired hands as they eat their dinner. In the best genteel tradition, Alexandra assumes the role of gracious hostess, not talking much, but encouraging "her men to talk." She listens "attentively, even when they [seem] to be talking foolishly" (53). In Alexandra's bearing and manner we are reminded of Cather's mother, Virginia Boak Cather.

We are told that the three young Swedish girls who tend to the cooking and housework are there because they afford Alexandra "a great deal of entertainment" and that, indeed, she could do the work herself "if it were necessary" (51). The point, of course, is that her newly acquired wealth and position have rendered physical labor allocatable. Alexandra has paid for the girls' fare in return for their services and loyalty. The young women remain in service until they marry, then are "replaced by sisters or cousins from the old country" (62). The implication is that the Swedish girls are "bound" servants, much like Marjorie Anderson was to the Cather family, and although Alexandra assures us of her fondness for these girls, the casual use of the word "replaced" does seem to suggest their expendability. Still, her loyalty to her own people is evident through her generosity in extending them an opportunity to come to the New World.

Likewise, her "noblesse oblige" extends to Ivar, who has lost his land. She offers him room and board in exchange for his wise counsel and small services: usually hitching up the horses and driving her wagon for her. Ivar, once an independent landowner, now bows "humbly" in her presence, protected by her "great prosperity" (55–56). He calls her "mistress" as do the servant girls. When Alexandra's servant Signa marries Nelse, Ivar loads their wedding presents into the wagon and drives "the bride and groom up to their new home, on Alexandra's northern quarter" (132), a scene not only reminiscent of the English landed gentry and their tenant farmers but also suggestive of Raymond Williams's concept of the neopastoral: an ideological vision of "agrarian capitalism" linked with the country house and its estate.[22] Moreover, Signa's devotion to her "mistress" is symbolically portrayed, through its biblical imagery, when she gives Alexandra a hot footbath, an act duplicated by the bound servant Mandy in "Old Mrs. Harris" and by the black slave Till in *Sapphira and the Slave Girl.*

Such class consciousness is further evident in the narrator's reference to John Bergson's wife, whom we know only as "Mrs. Bergson." We are told that although he "had married beneath him . . . he had married a good housewife" (17). John Bergson's dream is to make a fortune so that he might pay back those in the old country who had lost their money because of his father's business dealings. Once a wealthy man, his father had "married an unscrupulous woman" (137) and fallen prey to her corrupting influence.

In some ways, John Bergson and his wife seem to personify the dilemma of the postbellum South. John Bergson, a son of a once wealthy

CATHER'S NEW WORLD PASTORALS

family, has lost his inheritance through the mistakes of his father, ends in debt and despair, yet still hopes to reclaim the land. Mrs. Bergson, unable to let go of the past, holds on to the old traditions. She has "never quite forgiven John Bergson for bringing her to the end of the earth;"—a sentiment shared by both Willa Cather and her mother Virginia—but thinks only of reconstructing "her old life in so far as that [is] possible" (18). She survives, as does Cécile Auclair's mother in *Shadows on the Rock,* by recreating her orderly domestic world. Her "unremitting efforts to repeat the routine of her old life among new surroundings" does much "to keep the family from disintegrating morally and getting careless in their ways" (17). She creates beautiful flower gardens, orchards, and vegetable gardens, eking out of the barren soil the first seeds of the New Eden. But while her creative force seems to have much to teach Alexandra, she is ultimately as expendable as the Swedish servant girls. We barely notice her absence after Part One, told only that she now lies in a grave beside her husband.

But although John Bergson's paternal inheritance has been lost to him, he does bequeath his own land to his daughter and sons, fulfilling "the patrilineal inheritance of land" that Cather connected with "the hierarchies in Virginia's 'old conservative society.' "[23] Thus Alexandra, by Part Two, has become one of Randall's "natural aristocrats," one of the "up and coming on the Divide" (67). As Carl tells Alexandra, "One only has to drive through this country to see that you're all as rich as barons" (66). Moreover, Alexandra's brother Emil is now attending school to study law, a profession that will establish him as a member of the leisure class. Alexandra eschews the standards of the nouveau riche (as did Cather), choosing to keep much of the old furniture from their first home but allowing the local furniture dealer to decorate her dining room because "her guests liked to see about them these reassuring emblems of prosperity" (58).

Alexandra's perception of this new-found Eden, in which wealth is seen as a gift of nature, is reminiscent of William Byrd's Virginia plantation, where he tells us that he abounds "in all kinds of provisions without expense. . . . Like one of the patriarchs, I have my flock and herds, my bondmen and bondwomen, and every sort of trade amongst my own servants, so that I live in a kind of independence on everyone but Providence."[24] Likewise, her attitude echoes Michael Drayton's mythopoeic pastoral vision in "To the Virginian Voyage," a Golden Age where the abundance of nature provides for all without need of physical labor:

Where Nature hath in store
Fowle, Venison, and Fish,
    And the fruitfull'st Soyle
    Without your Toyle
Three Harvests more,
All greater then your Wish.[25]

When Carl asks Alexandra how she and her neighbors have accomplished their New Eden, she replies:

"We hadn't any of us much to do with it, Carl. The land did it. It had its little joke. It pretended to be poor because nobody knew how to work it right; and then, all at once, it worked itself. It woke up out of its sleep and stretched itself, and it was so big, so rich, that we suddenly found we were rich, just from sitting still." (69)

The irony, of course, rests in the physical and emotional toll extracted during those sixteen years between Carl's departure from the Divide and Alexandra's economic success, which Cather chooses not to share with the reader.

Reflecting the European vision of the New World, Alexandra's New Eden is orderly, symmetrical, and ostensibly solid and secure. But in the Virgilian pastoral tradition, death and tragic loss also reside in Arcady.[26] With the deaths of her brother Emil and Marie, Alexandra must accept, as Susan Rosowski points out, "that possession is impossible, of people and of the land."[27] People come and go, but the land remains. For all her desire to fulfill her father's Old World belief in acquiring land, Alexandra begins to understand that such ownership is at best tentative. Her realization that land is owned only "for a little while" by "people who love it and understand it" (179) suggests an emotional link to the previous tenants, the indigenous people who inhabited the plains and who could not comprehend "ownership" of the land.

Although Cather makes no allusions to Native Americans in her first plains novel, she does incorporate ancient indigenous civilizations in her next novel, *The Song of the Lark*. Considered the most autobiographical of her novels, *Song* tells the story of a young artist's struggle for and subsequent achievement of fame and fortune. According to David Stouck, *Song* is "a particular form of pastoral—a *künstlerroman*—in which childhood memories form a decisive aspect of the artist's growth to maturity."[28] But elements of the Virgilian pastoral also appear in many of the scenes or through Cather's stories within stories. For example, Ray Kennedy is originally a shepherd who, having lost his flock, becomes a railroad employee, only to be destroyed by the very mechanized world to which he had turned. The Mexican village on the outskirts of Moonstone likewise takes on pastoral overtones with its depiction of a simpler life.

The pastoral also is evident in Cather's idealization of ancient Native American civilizations. On the one hand Thea's later sojourn into Panther Cañon is mystical in its intuitive revelations. But it is also pastoral in its idealization of the past. Hers is an artistic revelation that links together past and present cultures, though entirely different, in an ongoing chain of creation and artistic vision. Hence, just as Cather drew upon ancient Rome and Greece for her heroic pastoral vision, she likewise turned to another ancient civilization, this time the Cliff Dwellers,[29] for her artistic vision.

Unlike Ray Kennedy, Tom Outland, or old Henry Biltmer (who maintains the ranch in Panther Cañon for Fred Ottenburg's father), Thea Kronborg makes a point of not disturbing any of the artifacts she discovers in Panther Cañon. When she does take a few pieces of the potsherds back to her lodging, she feels guilty, subsequently hiding the fragments under her bed.[30] She prefers to see herself as "a guest in these houses" (274). But although she does not attempt to take these artifacts for profit, she inadvertently appropriates something at least as valuable: their history. Thea's experience may in part be a turning "away from the romantic dreams of selfhood . . . a process of sympathy"[31] for another people, but the true center of Thea's mystical episode is the growth of the artist. History is transformed by her mythopoeic appropriation and imaginative interpretation of the lives of the ancient ones.

Just as she interpreted the immigrant experience in her earlier works, drawing on the pastoral tradition, Cather now envisioned a pastoral chapter in Native American history. Thea Kronborg's empathic and intuitive symbiosis with the artistic women of that ancient culture appears as a bonding over time, linking her to "a long chain of human endeavor" (275). Standing inside a cliff dwelling, Thea flicks a piece of carbon, the cooking smoke of the ancient ones, from the ceiling. "They were that near!" (271). She imagines them as "timid nest-building folk, like the swallows" (271). She begins "to have intuitions about the women who had worn the path" (271) and attempts to imitate their walk, feeling "the weight of an Indian baby" on her back. She hears a "voice out of the past" (271), senses the houses she enters are "haunted by certain fears and desires; feelings about warm and cold and water and physical strength" (272), believes she has acquired "a certain understanding of those old people" (272). Inspired by old Henry Biltmer's stories of the ancient ones, stories he has learned from the Pueblos, Thea's mythopoeic vision of the cañon takes on a ritualistic quality. In a symbol of rebirth, she bathes in the pool at the bottom of the cañon. The stream suggests to her "a continuity of life that reached back into the old time" (273). Yet, although she can envision the connecting threads of time, Thea never acknowledges individual human responsibility in the historic drama, what Robert Penn Warren calls "the awful responsibility of Time."[32] Thea may have learned, as Cass Mastern does in Warren's *All the King's Men,* that "the world is all of one piece . . . like an enormous spider web,"[33] but fails to see the connection between her presence in the cañon, now owned by Fred Ottenburg's father, and the displacement of the present-day descendants of the "ancient ones" she admires. By telling us Panther Cañon had been "deserted for hundreds of years when the first Spanish missionaries came to Arizona" (268), she exonerates the Europeans from playing any part in the extinction of this ancient civilization. For Cather, writing about the Navajos living on reservations in the early twentieth century would have been synonymous with writing about the situation of African Americans in the South during the same period, and both would require, not the mythopoeic, romanticized version, as with the ancient ones, but an honest, hard look at reality. This, however, was not Cather's intent, hence her choice of the ancient Cliff Dwellers and their culture as her subject. Her purpose was not to make a political statement, although she has been widely criticized for this omission, but to find an adequate trope for her art.[34]

Appropriating for her own Henry's tale of the clever ancient native

CATHER'S NEW WORLD PASTORALS

women who made vessels to hold precious water, Thea not only draws personal power from the story but also subsequently transforms the image into a metaphor for art: "what was any art but an effort to make a sheath, a mould in which to imprison for a moment the shining, exclusive element which is life itself" (273). More particularly, it becomes a trope for her own art: "In singing, one made a vessel of one's throat and nostrils and held it on one's breath" (273). Far from losing herself in the mystical experience, Thea's entire focus is on the artist within, stirring, though not yet born. In this gestation period, nestled in the womb-like caves of the Cliff Dwellers, she re-visions the historic past to suit her needs. Her mythopoeic visions nurture this unborn seed. The act is intentionally self-centered and fully consistent with Cather's concept of the heroic, struggling artist; with Dr. Archie's advice to Thea to forget the tramp and forge ahead; with the narrator's comments on the "common people"; with the Kohlers' prized "piece-picture" of Napoleon, which they later give to Thea; with Thea's photograph of the bust of Julius Caesar she keeps in her room in Chicago; and with her passion for reading about great generals. In the end, her inner conquest complete, Thea emerges as one of Cather's artistic aristocrats.

In her third, and perhaps best-known plains novel, *My Ántonia*, Willa Cather returns to the setting of *O Pioneers!* and with it to her previous vision of expansionism and the heroic pioneer. Curiously, her interest in the "ancient ones" that figured so prominently in *The Song of the Lark* all but vanishes from her next novel, leaving us to wonder why, if she had truly been moved by earlier Native American cultures, she continued to exclude their descendants' story from the concurrent one of United States expansionism. Yet her decision appears to be consistent with her pastoral vision. When Thea ponders what happened to the ancient ones, she does not have to confront the knowledge that her own people might have been responsible for the demise of the Cliff Dwellers because their civilization had already disappeared hundreds of years before the Europeans came to North America. But such was not the case for the white population that settled in Nebraska following the Civil War. They built their towns, cities, and railroads displacing native populations who were forced farther and farther northwest and eventually restricted to reservations. To tell this story concomitantly with the quest of the pioneers would be to tarnish the heroic vision. Faced with the same paradox as the Southern writers—the incompatibility of exploitation and displacement of the Other with the myth of New World democracy—Cather chose to exclude the story of these Native American tribes in *My Ántonia* just as she had in *O Pioneers!*, thus privileging the pastoral myth of the New Eden over historical fact. But Jim Burden's story, unlike Alexandra Bergson's and Thea Kronborg's, takes on a new ironic dimension.

In *Song*, Cather had begun to acknowledge the existence of racial prejudice in her pastoral domain, particularly in the attitudes of the townspeople toward the Mexicans. Thus she had begun to question the sincerity and validity of her pastoral vision. For perhaps the first time, she was confronted with the dilemma facing the Southern writers of this era: how to incorporate the, at times, violent, oppressive reality into the pastoral ideal. Her response was to continue to create her pastoral visions but through a juxtaposition of opposites, to create a historical context that functions as an antipastoral subtext, one that affords her readers alternative interpretations of the pastoral myths.

# 3

## The Pangs of Disillusionment
### Cather's Antipastoral Subtext

> ... poetry of the pastoral embraces both longing and
> wish-fulfillment. ... Poetry, however, is not only the
> child of fancy, but also the daughter of memory; and
> this makes her the sister of history.
> —Renato Poggioli, "The Oaten Flute"

L ewis P. Simpson, writing about antebellum Southern writers, suggests that their retreat into the pastoral mode in the form of the plantation narrative, which served as an antidote to an increasingly industrialized world, led to their alienation, a "withdrawal from memory and history."[1] By contrast, the Southern writers of the Reconstruction period who, although continuing to perpetuate the plantation pastoral myth, were more influenced by Virgil's *Eclogues* than by the myth of New World redemption. Rather than write of the harmonies of plantation life, they wrote of their loss, of "a land of dreams threatened by extinction."[2]

By the 1920s, the emphasis in Southern literature was still on the agrarian way of life rather than on modern industrialization. But according to Simpson, it had resulted in a "culture of alienation." Simpson does not discount the universality of modern alienation, a condition in opposition to the dehumanizing effects of a mechanized society. In the South, however, the reaction to what Simpson terms the "culture of alienation" was a call by some, namely those in the Agrarian movement, to restore "the pastoral mode of existence represented by an idealized

Old South," an agricultural society.[3] Thus the Southern writers of the 1920s and 1930s sought on the one hand to restore their past, to reify, in some ways, as did the Agrarians, the pastoral myth of a harmonious agricultural society, while on the other hand simultaneously attempting to recover their history. As Simpson notes, "The Southern literary mind which once had sought to symbolize its opposition to modernity in an image of pastoral permanence now began to seek to symbolize this antagonism in an image of a recovery—a restoration, perhaps a reconstruction—of memory and history."[4] Just as the later Southern writers of the 1920s and 1930s sought to restore history and memory, Cather had similarly begun to sense this estrangement from historical truth and the ensuing repercussions of alienation, what Susan Rosowski calls Cather's sensitivity "to feelings we term modern: a sense of alienation and historical discontinuity."[5]

Between the writing of The Song of the Lark and My Ántonia, a subtle change began to take place in Willa Cather's pastoral vision, a change that suggests her Southern sensibility had become more attuned to the dark underside of history. Although she had begun to address cultural, religious, and racial prejudices in her earlier work, most notably in Song, Cather was confronted, during the writing of My Ántonia in 1917 with the actual, inevitable consequence of rigid nationalism and hatred: a world war on a scale never before imagined. The war, as Elizabeth Shepley Sergeant recalls, "tore her apart . . . and loomed to her historic sense as the most important event since the French Revolution."[6] While Cather wrote the pastoral scenes in My Ántonia at her summer retreat in Jaffrey, New Hampshire, her "historic sense" was equally busy.

What had begun to change, I believe, is Cather's perception of "the beautiful past."[7] Literally confronted with history in the making and in its most violent form, Cather could no longer look to the past without seeing some of the reality of the present. Her heroic pioneer aristocracy had played an enormous role in the development of the West and in helping to usher in the industrial age. Now the industrial age was giving birth to weapons on a scale thus far unknown to man.

On the one hand Cather's response to this paradox was to continue glorifying the past, while seeming to suppress any potential inner conflict. Just as her grandmother Boak had condemned slavery but supported the institutions that sustained a slave society, not the least of which was the Confederate Army, Cather, seemingly unaware of any contradiction, continued to mythologize a past that had sanctioned conquest and exploitation. One thinks of Faulkner's Hightower who recalls how his grandfather disapproved of slavery, "The very fact that he could and did see no paradox in the fact that he took an active part in a partisan war and on the very side whose principles opposed his own, was proof enough that he was two separate and complete people, one of whom dwelled by serene rules in a world where reality did not exist."[8] On the other hand, Cather, herself "two separate and complete people," while continuing to idealize the past in her treatment of history, also gave a subtextual voice to her "historical sense." She succeeded, as did many of the Southern writers of this period, in creating an undertone of irony that was derived from the juxtaposition of myth and history.

This antipastoral subtext, juxtaposed against the pastoral myth, provides us with a historical context enabling us to experience opposing views. She creates her subtext within her historical allusions and references, allowing them to give voice to "the thing not named, of the overtone divined by the ear but not heard by it, the verbal mood, the emotional aura of the fact or the thing or the deed" (WCW 41–42). In other words, as Cather explains in her landmark essay "The Novel Démeublé," "Whatever is felt upon the page without being specifically named there—that, one might say, is created" (41). Through her historical allusions, she opens a window for us, allowing us to see beyond the mythopoeic visions of her characters to other interpretations of historical events. As Jo Ann Middleton notes, "Because Cather sees a work of art as a whole, we are well advised to regard the details and the gaps of juxtaposition as part of the whole."[9] This is not to say that Cather does not continue to privilege the mythical over the historical. Her position from the beginning of her career had always been the creation of art above all else. As she asserted in "The Novel Démeublé," "If the novel is a form of imaginative art, it cannot be at the same time a vivid and brilliant form of journalism" (WCW 40).

Cather's technique of juxtaposing opposites, as Merrill Maguire Skaggs points out, is particularly evident in her fourth novel My Ántonia.[10] Thus, while Ántonia embodies the pastoral vision, Jim Burden becomes a product of the modern industrial age. In her previous two novels, Cather created pastoral retreats for her central protagonists. Alexandra Bergson succeeds in achieving her agrarian Eden and Thea Kronborg discovers her artistic center, although both, in the tradition of the Virgilian pastoral, also suffer loss. Cather likewise simulates pastoral possibilities for Jim Burden and Niel Herbert, but then perversely denies them access to her fictional Arcady.

Always seeking new effects through her use of juxtapositions and contiguous opposites, Cather creates an ironic tension in *My Ántonia* and *A Lost Lady* through the juxtaposition of pastoral myth and history. Certainly the pastoral ideals, so much a part of her literary imagination, take on a different dimension in these novels. As Harold E. Toliver contends, the modern pastoralist, "aware of pastoral's artifice and of the contrast between fiction and reality . . . is likely to take a skeptical view of the pastoral tradition and use it primarily as a device for gaining perspective on the nature of the imagination itself."[11] While Cather does not necessarily take a skeptical view, she was certainly attuned to the ironic possibilities that "pastoral's artifice" afforded the writer.

Thus, through the characters of Jim Burden and Niel Herbert, we glimpse the mythmaking process, as well as their selection and rejection of historical evidence, and the ironies created by their choices. Both of these characters, like Cather herself, are drawn to a heroic ideal, an ideal, as William Empson has noted, often closely linked to the pastoral vision.[12] Jim Burden creates a mythopoeic narrative, transforming Ántonia into an archetypal earth goddess—the new Eve reclaiming her garden. But he remains an outsider, permitted only a temporary visit into her fruitful world. Niel Herbert fabricates heroic images of Captain Forrester and his wife, but he can never join their world as he envisions it.

Both of these characters are disconnected from the rush of life going on around them by their own fiction. Unlike Virgil's Meliboeus, who has been physically exiled from his homeland, Cather's characters have been more than physically displaced; they have been psychologically and emotionally exiled as well. They are both the dispossessed and the dispossessor, generating their own usurpation. Having come to a boundary, they are not so much expelled from their Arcady as excluded by a disenchantment with the fragile illusions of their youth. By choosing the illusion, the aesthetic ideal, over the grimmer historical amalgams, each of these men sets himself outside the bonded human community. Both Jim Burden and Niel Herbert fail at intimate relationships, and both, like Godfrey St. Peter and Myra Henshawe in Cather's later books, have severed their own ancestral roots. Each suffers, to varying degrees, the emotional pangs and emptiness of disillusionment. Similar to the Southern writers of the Reconstruction era, these characters are unable to acknowledge the sins of the fathers, and thus, alienated from blood ties, they experience a kind of historical anemia.

Our ideological heritage, according to Louis Althusser, exists before our birth, beginning with the patriarchal surname awaiting us. The existing cultural institutions of family, religion, education, law, political systems, and art enclose us in established, unexamined paradigms and presuppositions that determine our place in the world.[13] For Cather, that ideological heritage contained, among other things, the antebellum Southern myths, most of which have long since been dispelled by historians: the Cavalier Legend as the central origin of antebellum culture, the Plantation Legend spun from idealized illusions of grace and beauty, of benevolent master and loyal slave,[14] and later, legends of the brave Confederate soldiers who fought to preserve a way of life. In time the myth would expand to include those Southerners who joined the migrating forces moving West to conquer new territory, thus regenerating the myth of the New World.[15] If the Cavalier died at Gettysburg, he could be resurrected in a another form: the pioneer aristocrat,[16] the valiant conqueror of the new wilderness. If the gracious, elegant Plantation world had been left in cinders and shambles it, too, could rise again—mirrored in the aesthetic values and gracious lifestyles of wealthy bankers, landowners, and railroad barons: the new Western elite.

Both Jim Burden and Niel Herbert descend from Southern families. They embody these Southern aristocratic sensibilities within their attitudes and ideals, thus exemplifying an ideology similar to Cather's, one that incorporates gentility, aesthetic values and tastes, and an admiration for idealized beauty and for glorified conquest. Godfrey St. Peter, although not a Southerner, likewise exhibits an elitism similar to Jim's and Niel's in *The Professor's House*. All three characters, as Patricia Lee Yongue points out, share a "love of the pastoral and distaste for the modern materialistic life," which does not "preclude their fundamental, aristocratic worldliness."[17] But although Cather shares many of these traits with her characters, she intermittently judges these men harshly— particularly Jim Burden and Niel Herbert—often exposing their elitism and narrow views.

Finally, both of these men experience the pastoral longing for their lost youth. Jim Burden relives his past through his manuscript recounting his memory of Ántonia Shimerda, and Niel Herbert longs for the Golden Age of the pioneer aristocracy that he has idealized from his childhood perceptions.

All of these elements—class consciousness, hero-worship, and lost youth—are integrated into the pastoral modes of these two novels. Yet juxtaposed with these pastoral elements are the historical events that subtextually disclose another side of the story. While Cather establishes a pastoral vision within her protagonists, her textual allusions suggest an alternative version. By creating a historical antipastoral, Cather invites her readers to explore the factual dimensions behind the myths. Perhaps, after all, space could not redeem her from the "awful responsibility of Time." For although Cather's artistic sensibility privileged the pastoral myth over historical fact, her dichotomous nature also sought release in acknowledging the factual. Thus she welds these paradoxical views—two sides of one coin—asking us to contemplate both. While her Southern counterparts struggled with the pastoral distortions of their historical past, Cather began juxtaposing pastoral and heroic myths with subtextual clues to the historical reality, a fine balancing act that would eventually culminate in *My Mortal Enemy* with Myra Henshawe's confession that blood ties—and by implication, historical responsibility—are inescapable.

Myra's painful acknowledgment seems to be Cather's as well,[18] for Cather's Southern sensibility and fragments of her own familial history inform both *My Ántonia* and *A Lost Lady.* Therefore, in order to understand how Cather both employs and counters the pastoral in her work and how she elects to treat historical data, we must examine how her sociocultural background informs these two works. For the purpose of clarity, I will address this background in part one of this chapter; in part two, I will examine Cather's juxtaposition of the pastoral myth with historical data.

*I*

*My Ántonia* is replete with autobiographical references to Cather's own early years in Nebraska.[19] Jim's narration, although a fictionalized account, still captures much of the Southern culture through his depiction of his grandparents. For Paul Olson, these traits include "the Southern tradition of courtesy and distance, the simultaneous respect for and condescension toward other cultures (particularly black culture), the Virginia Baptist tradition to which the Burdens belong, and traditional southern classicism."[20]

Just as Virgil relates the stories of Arcady's exiles in his *Eclogues,* Jim Burden, a student of the classics, writes from the position of the privileged, educated class about those who labor in the soil and who are unable to write about their own experience. William Empson contends that it is impossible for the artist to empathize fully with his working-class subject because "the artist never is at one with any public ('I am in one way better, in another not so good')."[21] The relationship is that "of the complex man to the simple one."[22] Yet the artist/observer is, as is Jim Burden, always the outsider. Jim's appropriation of Ántonia's story is more than an aesthetic and mythopoeic rendering of Ántonia as the epitome of pioneer womanhood, as earth mother, or fertility goddess: it is also decidedly political.

Katrina Irving suggests that Jim, a white, middle-class Protestant male, narrating from a privileged position, not only endeavors to mold Ántonia, his "foreign, dark, Catholic" female antithesis, into his preconceived image of an American, but he also controls her story.[23] In the pastoral sense, the issue of control is perceived as bringing everything and everyone into a preconceived order. Ántonia's "place" in such a scheme is that of the servant girl, a condition arranged, albeit with ostensibly good intentions, by Jim's grandmother and sanctioned by Jim's hearty approval; although he later reveals that no matter what dire straits a "Pennsylvanian or Virginian found himself" in, he would never "let his daughters go into service" (128).

Several critics have noted the use of the possessive pronoun in the title, raising the issue of ownership. As Elizabeth Harrison points out, Southern women in the male Southern pastoral plot are always associated with the land and therefore with the property of the landowner. Southern women were either idealized or denigrated symbolically to represent virginal or despoiled land.[24] Thus the rape scene is often central to the male Southern pastoral.[25] The rape of a woman is synonymous with loss of land. Not surprisingly, Ántonia Shimerda, for Southern-born Jim Burden, is equated with the land. While not owned outright, she is nevertheless considered the property of several of the book's characters: her brother Ambrosch, Jim Burden, the Harlings, and the sinister Wick Cutter, who will attempt to fulfill the male Southern pastoral rape plot.

But in one of her typical reversals, and obviously aware of this literary devise, Cather alters the pastoral rape plot by having Jim Burden take Ántonia's place. When Wick Cutter slips into Ántonia's bedroom he is startled to find only Jim Burden in the young woman's bed. The situation leaves Jim deeply shaken and angry at Ántonia for exposing him to "all this disgustingness" (159). Cather seemingly turns the tables on her Southern male protagonist who, in using the possessive "my" when referring to Ántonia, exemplifies the Southern pastoral vision of women as "property."

The pastoral myth of the New World is further represented in the town of Black Hawk. Not only does the narrator refer to it as "the new world" (94) but depicts it as the status quo: "a clean, well-planted little prairie town, with white fences and good green yards about the dwellings, wide dusty streets, and shapely little trees growing along the wooden sidewalks" (94). Black Hawk is the raw, barren plains transformed under the civilizing forces of Western European culture, and it is into this world that Ántonia is conditionally invited.

With Ántonia firmly entrenched in the Harling household nearby, Jim can keep a steady eye on her behavior, as do most of the townsfolk. Both Jim's grandmother and Mrs. Harling believe Ántonia needs a civilizing force in her life. Here in Black Hawk such benevolent meddling is not conveyed as the busybody machinations of Moonstone's Mrs. Livery Johnson in *Song* or Skyline's Mrs. Jackson in "Old Mrs. Harris" because the target is not the narrator or the character from whose point of view we experience the story but rather the Other. In Black Hawk, acceptance by the community means adjusting one's behavior to accommodate the status quo. Ántonia herself acknowledges this unspoken rule and the lessons of these early civilizing forces years later when she tells Jim that she

"Learned nice ways at the Harlings' " and that without such knowledge she would probably have raised her children "like wild rabbits" (221).

But Jim, too, is not exempt from small town pressures to conform. Mrs. Harling does not understand why Jim prefers the company of the hired girls over "the girls of [his] own set" (146). His Baptist grandmother asks him to give up going to the public dances he enjoys because "People say [he is] growing up to be a bad boy" (145). Jim has few illusions about the narrow conventions of small-town living. Pacing up and down the dark streets, looking at the houses, he observes, "The life that went on in them seemed to me made up of evasions and negations; shifts to save cooking, to save washing and cleaning, devices to propitiate the tongue of gossip. This guarded mode of existence was like living under a tyranny. People's speech, their voices, their very glances became furtive and repressed. Every individual taste, every natural appetite, was bridled by caution" (140).

Along with the narrow vision of the townsfolk, individual prejudices and elements of nationalism pervade the pages of *My Ántonia*. Cather was well aware of these prejudices and, as Woodress has noted, took deep offense to the treatment of the immigrants.[26] She was particularly disturbed by the way many of the Virginians who had moved to Nebraska viewed the immigrant populations. Her acute observations of these prejudices are evident in her portrayal of her characters, through whom she exposes the narrowness of their views. Jake believes he will contact diseases from the "foreigners" (6). Jim's grandmother speaks to the immigrants as if they are deaf. Jim notes Ambrosch has shrewd eyes, "like his mother's, but more sly and suspicious" (17). Otto, who is Austrian, comments on the Bohemians' "natural distrust of Austrians" (16). Distrust is also evident in Jake's and Jim's attitudes. Following a confrontation with Ambrosch, his mother, and Ántonia, Jake reminds Jim, "These foreigners ain't the same. You can't trust 'em to be fair. . . . They ain't to be trusted" (84). Jim responds in kind, "I believe they are all like Krajiek and Ambrosch underneath" (84), a judgment based on two immigrant men he dislikes. And later Otto, witnessing Ántonia's verbal retaliation, simply remarks, "You can't tell me anything new about a Czech; I'm an Austrian" (85).

As a Southern family uprooted from their native Virginia and transported to the barren plains of Nebraska, the Burdens bring with them their inherent prejudices as well as their customs and manners. Thus, even while Jim's grandmother looks down on Mrs. Shimerda and her ways, she and Jake discuss how important it is for good Christian people to remember "they were their brothers' keepers" (52). Always aware of the need to show respect and good manners, the grandmother, in the midst of the Shimerdas' hovel, goes on "talking in her polite Virginia way, not admitting their stark need or her own remissness" (49) in not coming to their aid sooner. Hence there is a general distrust among the immigrants toward native-born Americans and established immigrants as well. Mrs. Shimerda clearly blames Jim's grandmother for not doing enough to help them in their need, and Mr. Shimerda is angered by Krajiek's unfair treatment of his family.

Grandmother Burden believes she has "saved" Ántonia by placing her in a nice home where she might learn good manners. But implicit in her generous act is perhaps also the need to help Ántonia in her assimilation into American culture, and away from her own Eastern European heritage, which by Black Hawk's standards (as Jim Burden knows, and Cather herself knew) is considered by the townspeople as less acceptable, a truth not lost on Ántonia. "Maybe I be the kind of girl you like better, now I come to town" (100), she tells Jim's grandmother.

As in *My Ántonia*, Cather's Southern sensibility permeates the pages of *A Lost Lady*, published five years later.[27] Like Ántonia, Marian Forrester is the focus of youthful male adoration. On the surface, she is Cather's Midwestern version of a Southern belle. She is a charming hostess, flirtatious, disarming in her deference to the Captain's male guests, and a woman of taste and culture. Although this novel is set in the small town of Sweet Water, Colorado, the attitudes of the townspeople, the depiction of the immigrant population, and the rendering of the landscape are all similar to Cather's Red Cloud (a.k.a. Moonstone, Black Hawk, and Skyline). Niel Herbert is the progeny of Kentucky parents, but unlike Jim Burden, who was born in Virginia, it is not clear whether he was born in Sweet Water or in Kentucky, later migrating West with his family. Like Cather, Niel's Southern attitudes have been instilled in him by his parents, and by his uncle, Judge Pommeroy. Niel—whose youthful, idealistic vision often distorts his judgment—sees the vibrant, gracious Mrs. Forrester and the heroic Captain Forrester as representative of an aesthetic ideal, one that is threatened by changing values in an increasingly modernized industrial world.

It seems apparent that on some level Cather had the Old South in mind when she wrote *A Lost Lady.* The book may even be read as an allegory of the postbellum era. The demise of the natural (pioneer) aristocrats (the Old Order)[28] at the hands of the new generation of materialists simulates post–Civil War Reconstruction. Captain Forrester, a Civil War veteran (we are never told on which side he fought), married to the young, vivacious Marian, a brilliant and charming hostess, patterned after the quintessential Southern lady, lives a gracious, genteel life in a large, elegant—though not particularly remarkable—house, a place known "for its hospitality and for a certain charm of atmosphere" (9). Just as the South suffered under Northern occupation and the scourge of ruthless carpetbaggers with Southerners facing financial ruin, the loss of their land, and ultimately their way of life, the Forresters, too, eventually face financial ruin, genteel poverty, and the loss of their aesthetic, cultured world.

Ivy Peters, an allegorical representation of the ruthless carpetbagger, metaphorically rapes the land (alters it for profit), and eventually possesses (defiles) the Captain's wife. Motivated by greed, Peters takes advantage of the Captain's financial misfortune by convincing him to rent the meadow: an edenic marsh, which has been a refuge to Marian Forrester, and a pastoral vision to Niel Herbert. Once the marsh is in his possession, Ivy Peters drains it in order to grow wheat for profit. And although the Captain has ostensibly rented the land for money, it seems evident that his purpose has more to do with financial survival than greed. Ivy Peters, however, has a more sinister motive. While profit is certainly a factor, he has more personal reasons. For in draining the marsh, he also takes satisfaction in destroying Marian's place of refuge. He is the New Order, the brazen insensible future of Sweet Water and the Midwest, the crass materialist of the modern industrial age that Cather abhorred. It must have seemed to her as if the tragedy of the Old South was being played out for a second time, now in the Midwest. All of her New World visions for a rebirth of a cultured society had begun to collapse under the direction of the unscrupulous men who served as the prototypes for Wick Cutter and Ivy Peters.

Niel Herbert's elitist vision—however negatively it sometimes emerges in Cather's hand—is also Cather's. He is her "artist/aristocrat" who, like Cather herself, possesses "a strong sense of order and beauty."[29] Orphaned and living with his uncle Judge Pommeroy since Niel's father had moved to Denver, and motherless since the age of five, Niel finds a surrogate family in the Forresters when, following the Captain's stroke, he becomes a regular visitor to their home. He makes himself virtually indispensable. During his nightly vigils, as he keeps watch over the couple, he feels a satisfaction in being surrounded by "the old things that had seemed so beautiful to him in his childhood" and acknowledges that "No other house could take the place of this one in his life" (142). While the orphaned Jim Burden sought family ties with immigrants, Cather— exploring yet another opposite—has Niel aspire to a family connection with the Forresters, people of position and wealth.[30]

Marian Forrester, the first of Cather's aristocratic women,[31] as many critics have noted, is modeled to some degree on Cather's own mother, indeed embodies many of the Southern belle qualities of Virginia Cather, although the actual prototype for Marian is the wife of Red Cloud's Silas Garber. As Merrill Skaggs points out, Marian's power is sexual. She controls the men in her life and draws the admiration of her husband, who acknowledges her power.[32] Her use of her sexuality links her to a long line of classic Southern belles who also understood the potency of such power. Yet, despite this control, the Captain also sees her, in the Southern male tradition, as his property. He tells his dinner guests the story of how he "planned to build a house that [his] friends could come to, with a wife like Mrs. Forrester to make it attractive to them" (53).

Captain Forrester, likewise, embodies traits of the Southern gentleman: an officer, a cultured host, a man who enjoys intelligent company and fine wine, and a member of the leisure class. When his bank faces ruin, the Captain, in the tradition of noblesse oblige, unlike the younger investors, is determined that none of the depositors "should lose a dollar" (90). The Poles, Swedes, and Mexicans to whom his name had "promised security and fair treatment" (90) are reimbursed by means of his own private fortune, leaving the Captain with only his house and a small income.

Other, though more subtle, references to the South or Southern way of life permeate the novel. They suggest parallels between the novel and

Cather's early childhood memories. Perhaps one of the less obvious allusions is to the willow stake the Captain uses to mark the land he will later purchase in Sweet Water. Cather links the antebellum era of her grandfather's Virginia home, Willow Shade, which was once surrounded by four stately willow trees, with Captain Forrester's pioneer achievements, when the Captain states, "I found my willow stake,—it had rooted and grown into a tree,—and I planted three more to mark the corners of my house" (54).

Perhaps one of the more unusual features of this novel is Cather's employment of Southern dialect. With the brief exception of Blind D'Arnault's dialogue in *My Ántonia,* Cather had not attempted Southern dialect since her earliest short stories. Her choice to do so in *A Lost Lady* suggests, once again, that the South was indeed on her mind when she wrote this story of the decline of the pioneer aristocracy. Both Mrs. Ogden, a Virginian, and her daughter Constance speak in Southern dialect. Furthermore, Judge Pommeroy, whose speech is predominantly formal, also lapses into dialect when he tells Marian Forrester the story of her husband's financial ruin: "But, 'pon my honour, I couldn't forbid him," he tells Mrs. Forrester following the Captain's decision to bail out his depositors using his personal wealth: "As for those white-livered rascals that sat there,—" (92). Perhaps even more revealing is the derogatory analogy the Judge employs to denounce the younger breed of businessmen: "In my day the difference between a business man and a scoundrel was bigger than the difference between a white man and a nigger" (92). The Judge's outburst over the Captain's situation, in fact, further signifies the parallels between that of the pioneer aristocracy and the Old South.

Cather's class consciousness also is evident in her rendering of the town's hierarchical structures. The social strata are established from the beginning: On the one hand we have "the homesteaders and hand-workers who were there to make a living"; on the other hand we have "the bankers and gentlemen ranchers who came from the Atlantic seaboard to invest money and to 'develop our great West' " (10). The latter inhabit the realm of "railroad aristocracy" (9), which includes Captain Forrester. That Cather envisioned an almost feudal society is suggested in the narrator's reference to "the lower world of Sweet Water" (14), a world inhabited by the butcher's son, the grocer's twins, the Blum boys (two sons of the German tailor), and Ed Elliott whose father owns a shoe store. The lower world is Niel Herbert's childhood domain, one from which he wishes to escape. He refers to his father's small house as "not a pleasant place to go; a frail egg-shell house, set off on the edge of the prairie where people of no consequence lived" (29). The Blum boys, in particular, recognize this feudal distinction, as they regard Marian Forrester "humbly from under their pale, chewed-off hair, as one of the rich and great of the world. They realized more than their companions, that such a fortunate and privileged class was an axiomatic fact in the social order" (19). When Adolph Blum happens upon Marian and her lover Frank Ellinger in the forest, the narrator informs us that it would never occur to the boy to betray Mrs. Forrester's secret. "His mind was feudal; the rich and fortunate were also the privileged" (68). His loyalty to Mrs. Forrester stems from her treatment of him as a "human-being" (68).

Niel's own class consciousness is also evident from the beginning. He is fully aware that his connection to Judge Pommeroy sets him a notch above the others and elicits more than the usual nod Mrs. Forrester reserves for the other boys. Although his father is "a gentle, agreeable man . . . with nice manners" (30), Niel feels an "air of failure and defeat about his family" (30) because his father has lost his property. He thinks of his Cousin Sadie, a poor relation who tends to the house (much as did the Cathers' bound servant Marjorie) as "a good-natured thing" (30) who is "probably the worst housekeeper in the world" (29). In fact, her housekeeping is so poor, he is embarrassed to have anyone visit his house. Little wonder, then, that he elects to live with Judge Pommeroy after his father moves away. His uncle is Niel's direct link to the Forresters.

Judge Pommeroy is a man of honor and dignity in the genteel tradition. A lawyer and a member of the leisure class, he conducts himself with noble bearing. But although he studied law at the University of Virginia, Cather never specifically identifies his Southern roots. We can assume because he is Niel's maternal uncle, that he, like Niel's mother, came West from Kentucky. Furthermore, his attitude toward blacks and his lapse into dialect, seem to corroborate his Southern heritage.

Black Tom, the Judge's "faithful Negro servant" (31), aside from filling a stereotypical role and aside from his assumed position as a free man, is still treated as a possession, an object to be passed around. Marian Forrester asks the Judge if he will "lend" her Tom to assist at her dinner party, as if he were a piece of furniture or an article of clothing. This view of person-as-object is further exemplified by Niel's request to his uncle to "let" him have Tom to help at the Forrester's after the Captain falls ill. We are then told "Tom was put in the kitchen" (140).

But Cather extracts a heavy price for Jim Burden's and Niel Herbert's elitist views and idealized perceptions, condemning them to a form of self-marginalization. Their dispossession is linked to their estrangement from history and historical continuity.

## II

Jim Burden and Niel Herbert are confronted with their pastoral ideals at a critical juncture in their lives. Both men, as previously noted, have incorporated the heroic ideal into their pastoral visions. Both, from a privileged position, in some way appropriate and ultimately mythicize the story of another person or persons, transforming the Other's story into a personal myth to conform to their inherent presuppositions. Both, in turn, must choose their own method of coping with knowledge that threatens their pastoral visions: Jim Burden and Niel Herbert elect to hold on to their myths, although it means living in emotional exile.

Neither Jim Burden nor Niel Herbert is endowed with a strong historical sense. Cather, herself, was first and foremost an artist. Although interested in history and careful in her research, she chose historical facts that would enhance her fictional narrative and support her pastoral ideal. It seems evident, however, that through these two characters, Cather had begun to explore the complex connections between myth and history.

History, as the new historicists have posited, consists not only of the events of the past but also of the interpretation of those events in narrative form. The past, therefore, can never be truly available to us as it actually happened. Thus, we are able to examine Cather's cultural and ideological presuppositions within the framework of her literary imagination, as well as through her selective use of history. For example, while the prejudices of the characters are intentionally and clearly defined in *My Ántonia,* other historical acts of aggression, exploitation, and dispossession are either totally absent from Jim's narrative or mythically transformed into transcendent images. Jim Burden shuns historical insight. His vision of Ántonia is a mythopoeic creation, as is much of his narrative.[33] On the one hand he controls Ántonia's story, but he also controls, through narrative, historical content. Nevertheless, the historical content has also previously been selected by Cather who, by intentionally placing it in the text, asks us to consider the factual data independent of Jim Burden's perceptions and misinterpretations.

The ancient native civilizations that figured so prominently in *Song* are only inadvertently alluded to in *My Ántonia*. As Mike Fischer notes, *My Ántonia* ignores the displacement of the Native Americans while heralding the establishment of white settlements in the West. The conflicts depicted here are between whites of different nationalities, not whites and native populations. This is "a story of origins for whites only." [34] But interwoven with the myths are decisive clues to the historical past. When Jim kills the rattlesnake, he tells Ántonia the snake's rattles indicate it was twenty-four years old, "that he must have been there when white men first came, left on from buffalo and Indian times" (32). Yet the opening passages of the book, like those of *O Pioneers!* depict an uninhabited, barren wilderness, "There was nothing but land: not a country at all, but the material out of which countries are made" (7). Jim's statement about "Indian times," a historical reality, contradicts the mythopoeic version he imparts to the reader at the beginning of the book. We learn, almost inadvertently, that it has been less than a mere twenty-odd years since the Indians inhabited this area. Implicit in this fact is the displacement of these same native cultures by white men. Moreover, prejudicial assumptions regarding these predecessors are evident in Jake and Otto's contention that the "great circle" where the Indians used to ride near Grandfather Burden's cornfield was the site of Indian atrocities. They are "sure that when they galloped round that ring the Indians tortured prisoners bound to a stake in the centre" (42). They continue to embrace this belief even though the grandfather claims the circle was probably used to run races and train horses.

Paul Olson's reading of *My Ántonia* compares the image of the plow—a heroic vision "black against the molten red" (*MA* 156) of the sun—with Aeneas's vision of the sword and shield with which he will forge the future of Rome, and with the vision of his bronze breastplate in the *Aeneid*.[35] The book's ending, which places Jim in the agrarian world of Ántonia's New Eden, and the image of the plow's disappearance into darkness suggest both the diminishment of male dominance

and military conquest and the rise of peace and prosperity within an
agrarian society,[36] as does Virgil's *Georgics,* with the juxtaposed images
of Caesar "launching the vast thunder of his war / Over the deep
Euphrates" and Virgil passing these "selfsame days . . . in sweet Parthe-
nope, . . . / Played with the shepherd's muse, and made [his] song / Of
Tityrus beneath the beech-tree's shade."[37] But Mike Fischer contends
that the reason for the plow's disappearance suggests a double loss of
both the pastoral vision and the heroic warrior epic.[38] Fischer perceives
the scene preceding Jim's observation of the plow as negating the georgic
vision. When Jim Burden relates the story of the Spanish sword found
in a farmer's field in a county north of his, and of Coronado's search
for the Seven Golden Cities (155), he is essentially relating—although
apparently unaware of it—a story of early conquest, greed, and atrocities
against native cultures.

Most revisionist historians have written extensively on this subject,
dispelling old myths of the "virgin land." But Jim's version is centered
on the heroic, the mythopoeic, not the mimetic. His is an imagined version of an event based on the presuppositions of his society. When the
hired girls, to whom he relates the story, want to know why Coronado
never returned to Spain, Jim tells them Coronado "died in the wilderness, of a broken heart" (155), a questionable fact he has learned from his
schoolbooks,[39] but contemporary sources suggest Coronado died "dis-
graced by his government for his inhumane treatment of New Spain's
native population."[40] As Fischer points out, the discrepancy between
Jim's textbook knowledge and the actual historical account suggests
Cather's knowledge of the Coronado expeditions may have exceeded
standard textual accounts.[41] She had, after all, spent considerable time in
the Southwest prior to writing *The Song of the Lark* and had felt a deep
affinity with the ancient native cultures. She had been especially fond of
her guide, Julio, from whom she learned local legends and folklore, and
she had spent considerable time learning about the country and the people from the local priest Father Connolly.[42] She was also inclined to read
whatever historical information she could find on places for which she
felt a special affinity. Moreover, in her later novel *Death Comes for the
Archbishop,* she includes accounts of Spanish mistreatment of the native
populations. Thus we may view Cather's reference to Coronado's sword
as an invitation to explore the historical reality outside of Jim's mytho-

poeic version. The pioneers, like their European ancestors traveling to the New World, had migrated West it seems, only to find their New Eden equally corrupted, and themselves once again tied inexorably to historical responsibility.

But whether we view *My Ántonia* as a pastoral of innocence, as David Stouck would have us do,[43] or as a pastoral in the tradition of Virgil's *Georgics*, as John Randall, Paul Olson, and others suggest, we cannot overlook the role that the adult Jim Burden has played in the destruction of the pastoral childhood vision he recounts in his narrative. A lawyer for "one of the great Western railways" (1), his position allies him with industry and modern progress and, by extension, with the displacement of indigenous populations as well as the destruction of his idyllic boyhood images. If, as Harold Toliver has pointed out, "a pastoral place indulges to celebrate nature rather than improve it,"[44] then Jim Burden has failed his own vision. The book opens with him heading West on a train, a metaphorical iron snake that wends its way through the New Eden, a world embodied in the image of Ántonia, a world that has already been irreparably altered by the presence of the railroad. Jim is, as John Murphy contends, "a symptom of the society he condemns, unwittingly condemning himself in the process."[45] Thus Cather establishes him as an antipastoral figure with, ironically, a pastoral sensibility.

Jim Burden's aesthetic vision, like Cather's, is frequently in conflict with his ideological position, a position distinctly linked with U.S. expansionist policy and the pioneers, thus producing a condition intellectually and psychologically equivalent to that of the antebellum Southern writers who risked their literary imaginations, their "independent minds," according to Lewis Simpson, to merge unsuccessfully the pastoral myth with the oppressive reality of their history.[46] As Blanche Gelfant points out, "*My Ántonia* is a magnificent and warped testimony to the mind's image-making power, an implicit commentary on how that creative power serves the mind's need to ignore and deny whatever is reprehensible in whatever one loves."[47]

Jim Burden, whose surname (anticipating that of Robert Penn Warren's Jack Burden) symbolically signifies his place in history and his inherent responsibility in the web of life, can only be a visitor in Ántonia's Eden. Unlike her, he is not a part of the natural world. The world he has chosen is urban, industrial, linear, and masculine. By contrast, Ántonia has reclaimed the land. Together they represent the pastoral opposites of rural and urban life. Thus it falls to Jim, as it did to Virgil, to tell the story of the heroic men and women who worked the soil.

Yet, for all his worldly success, Jim Burden seems disconnected, an outsider. From the beginning he is depicted as uprooted, exiled from his home state of Virginia, left with no other recourse than to live with his aging grandparents in Nebraska following the deaths of his parents. His initial displacement is involuntary, but his life thereafter seems to follow a pattern of self-marginalization, including his loveless relationship with his wife. When he returns to Black Hawk as an adult, Jim Burden recognizes no one in town. Those whom he had known in his youth have either died or moved away. Ántonia is the single connection to his "incommunicable past." For the past is indeed unknowable: an imaginative blend of historical events colored by human memory. Perhaps, then, Jim's insistent mythologizing of Ántonia's story, his continued belief in the pastoral ideal which he connects to her image, is what gives him a sense of continuity and order in the fast-paced industrialized world in which he has chosen to live.

Just as the aesthetic ideal is signified by Ántonia for Jim Burden, for Niel Herbert in *A Lost Lady*, it is embodied in the form of Marian Forrester and in the heroic vision of Captain Forrester. They fulfill his presuppositions regarding the pioneer aristocracy. Niel, as James Woodress points out, has been assigned the Arcadia theme. He never loses his belief "that the pioneer era was nobler and better than the present."[48]

As with Jim Burden, we must examine Niel's role in Cather's pastoral vision.[49] His pastoral world consists, among other things, of the marsh on the Forrester's property, a world of natural, untouched beauty, where he and his friends have spent much of their childhood. The scene in the marsh just prior to Niel's discovery of Marian's unfaithfulness to her husband is replete with an edenic innocence. The "fresh morning air" has "an almost religious purity" (84); the birds fly through "the unstained atmosphere" (85). Niel wonders why he doesn't visit the marsh more often during these peak morning hours "to see the day before men and their activities had spoiled it, while the morning was still unsullied, like a gift handed down from the heroic ages" (85). Upon discovering Marian's affair with Frank Ellinger, Niel's pastoral world crumbles: "the morning had been wrecked for him; and all subsequent mornings" (86).

Marian has destroyed an "aesthetic ideal" (87), an ideal that reaches beyond physical beauty to embrace Niel's vision of a heroic age. As in the male Southern pastoral, the fallen woman signifies the despoiled land, property stolen from its rightful owner. For Niel, Marian is a mere extension of the Captain and all his achievements; her disgrace sullies Captain Forrester, who is the true center of Niel's ideal. Yet it is the Captain who, having fallen on financially difficult times, rents the marsh to Ivy Peters with the full and practical knowledge of his intent to drain the marsh and plant wheat. Ivy Peters, however, rather than Captain Forrester, is the focus of Niel's scorn and contempt. From Niel's point of view, Ivy and the new, coarser generation are responsible for the destruction of former pastoral retreats, and a more gracious way of life, much as the postbellum South and its agrarian landscape were forever altered by the Northern industrialists. Niel, however, in his immature idealism remains historically blind to the Captain's own part in his downfall.

Recent scholars have begun to examine the process by which Cather's characters mythologize historical events within the narrative context of *A Lost Lady* and by which they transpose historical fact into myth for ideological purposes.[50] Niel Herbert mythologizes those historical events that might conflict with accepted cultural values. Unlike Cather, he has no historical point of reference. As Joseph Urgo notes, Niel has neither a "sense of historical time" nor "historical context."[51] Interwoven with Niel's limited historical perceptions are, I believe, what Cather designed as intentionally ambiguous narrative accounts, the stories within stories, which mythologize factual information in both fictional and historical contexts. They serve as a testimony to the power of the human imagination to reinvent history for its own ends. For example, Marian Forrester's "Once upon a time" (164) account of her rescue by Captain Forrester deliberately omits the scandalous episode that precedes it.

Similarly, Captain Forrester's account of how he came to build his home in Sweet Water is also an edited or revised version. He relates to his dinner guests his chance encounter with an Indian encampment located on a hill. "Greatly taken with the location" (52), he drives a willow stake in the ground, marking the spot to which he will later return to buy the land from the railroad. Two historical facts reside in his account: first, that the land has been occupied by Indians, and second, the railroad has acquired that land. Twelve years later the Captain builds his stately house and brings Marian Forrester, his second wife, to Sweet Water to grace his new home. The Captain then expands his narrative to include a discourse on his philosophy regarding the achievements of the pioneer aristocracy:

> "Well, then, my philosophy is that what you think of and plan for day by day, in spite of yourself, so to speak—you will get. . . . because a thing that is dreamed of in the way I mean is already an accomplished fact. All our great West has been developed from such dreams; the homesteader's and the prospector's and the contractor's. We dreamed the railroads across the mountains, just as I dreamed my place on the Sweet Water. All these things will be everyday facts to the coming generation, but to us—" Captain Forrester ended with a sort of grunt. Something forbidding had come into his voice, the lonely, defiant note that is so often heard in the voices of old Indians. (54–55)

The allusion to the "coming generation" is an obvious sore point with the Captain, as it is with Niel. The future, as the Captain and Niel both see it, lies in the hands of unscrupulous men like Ivy Peters. But what Niel fails to see are the historical parallels between the Captain and Ivy Peters. The latter is the natural heir to the former.[52] As a railroad man and contractor, the Captain has been at the forefront of U.S. expansionist policies that have resulted in uprooting and displacing entire native populations, at times by violent means. When the Captain speaks of the Indian encampment, he never tells us whether it was an abandoned camp or an inhabited one. What is clear, however, is the means by which he procures this land. He purchases the property from the railroad, which had acquired the land from the original inhabitants through questionable practices.

Thus, in juxtaposing the Captain's story with the historical details of the Indian encampment, with the railroad men and contractors dreaming their way West, and with his means of procuring the property, Cather invites us to examine not only the inner workings of the myth-making process but also the human capacity for self-deception. Had her intention merely been to perpetuate the existing myth, Cather would not have alluded to the Indian encampment. She would have created an uninhabited wilderness, as she did for Alexandra Bergson and Jim Burden, to suggest no one had set foot on the "virgin soil" before Captain For-rester. It seems especially poignant (and ironic), then, that Niel links the Captain's indignation over the unscrupulous practices of the "com-ing generation" with "the lonely, defiant note . . . heard in the voices of old Indians." The allusion suggests the Captain's awareness of how the events of history result in the displacement of cultures—the old order inevitably giving way to the new—in the ongoing human drama.

Ivy Peters, who later manages Marian's estate following the Captain's death, merely extends the practices set in motion by his pioneer prede-cessors. "He gets splendid land from the Indians some way, for next to nothing" (123), Marian tells Niel. Aware that Ivy's methods are undoubt-edly crooked, she asks Niel not to tell Judge Pommeroy, who once man-aged the Captain's affairs, justifying her decision by claiming the Judge's "methods don't work nowadays" (123). Marian's morally ambiguous out-burst—"I don't admire people who cheat Indians. Indeed I don't!" (124)—speaks for an entire society that voices verbal indignation while silently reaping financial benefits from those they verbally condemn. Marian herself is first married to a man who has inadvertently cheated Indians, and she then puts herself under the financial guidance of an-other one whom she knows to be doing so.

Niel may be appalled by Ivy Peter's questionable business practices, but he chooses not to see their origins. To do so would undermine his heroic vision of the pioneer age, an era already on the wane during his boyhood.

> This was the very end of the road-making West; the men who had put plains and mountains under the iron harness were old; some were poor, and even the successful ones were hunting for rest and a brief reprieve from death. It was already gone, that age; nothing could ever bring it back. The taste and smell and song of it, the visions those men had seen in the air and followed,—these he had caught in a kind of afterglow on their own faces,—and this would always be his. (168–69)

To Niel, these men were "great-hearted adventurers," members of a "courteous brotherhood," and "great land-holders" (106). He condemns Marian Forrester because she prefers "life on any terms" (169), yet he fails to see that the same credo was likewise the propelling force behind the pioneer expansion. Perhaps one of the stronger analogies to this moral ambiguity lies in Niel's account of Frank Ellinger, whose reputation for being "notoriously wild" includes the story—one of many—of Frank's daytime excursion with a prostitute. As Niel observes, "Morals were different in those days" (49). Even the women laugh over the stories of Frank's exploits, for although he is considered "terribly fast," he is nevertheless a devoted son, "caring for an invalid mother, . . . a combination" that "pleased the taste of the time. Nobody thought the worst of him" (50). Moral issues, then, are given a historical context, a temporal existence. Moreover, Niel's observations suggest a society that weighs these issues based on a system of justification, one that has been established within an ideological framework. In such a system, Niel can freely dismiss or choose to ignore the means by which the railroad aristocracy achieved its ends.

Niel Herbert's acceptance and perpetuation of the pioneer mythology serve only to alienate him from his present reality. As we have seen, Jim Burden cannot enter the New Eden he has envisioned for Ántonia because his historical position—that is, his professional position in conjunction with the modern industrial world—is in direct conflict with the interests of that pastoral garden. Similarly Niel Herbert is shut out of the gracious, cultured world of the noble pioneer aristocracy because in reality it does not, nor ever did, exist in the manner in which he has envisioned it. He is, in the end, the least connected character in the novel. Alone, without wife or family, his solution, like Jim Burden's, is to continue re-visioning the past to suit his aesthetic sensibility. When he hears, once more, about "his long-lost lady" (172), he discovers she had married a wealthy Englishman and lived quite happily until her death. The possessive "his," like Jim Burden's "My" when he refers to Ántonia, signifies possession only in the sense that both men have fashioned stories of women who, had they been able to tell their own, would have undoubtedly crafted very different accounts. In reality, Marian, a pragmatic survivor, is well-equipped to take care of herself in the real world, a characteristic Niel condemns. Because she "preferred life on any terms," because she would not "immolate herself, like the widow of all these great men," Niel holds a "weary contempt for her in his heart" (169). Her sin, it appears, is her refusal to perpetuate Niel's illusions to satisfy his aesthetic needs. His last words about Marian and her second husband are deliberately calculated to resurrect his earlier revered image of the flighty, vivacious woman who needed to be looked after: " 'So we may feel sure that she was well cared for, to the very end,' " he tells Ed Elliott. " 'Thank God for that!' " (174).

Neither Jim Burden nor Niel Herbert ever question their presuppositions within a historical context, choosing instead mythologized versions of past events, without regard to the psychological alienation their distortions have created. But Cather, herself struggling through a difficult psychological crisis,[53] continued to explore the dynamics of myth and history. In her attempts to sustain her heroic myths in the industrialized modern world, she became increasingly disillusioned, as is evident in *The Professor's House.*

In *The Professor's House,* Cather returns to the pastoral motif of idealizing "a golden age almost always associated with childhood,"[54] thus linking Godfrey St. Peter with Jim Burden and Niel Herbert who likewise view their childhood pasts as innocent and idyllic. He also shares their aesthetic sensibility. But unlike his two predecessors, St. Peter, the historian, does have a historical sense. In his aesthetic desire to immortalize his heroic vision, he has literally and figuratively been "keeping up two establishments" (271)—the historical and the mythical. The conflict has left him numb. Drained of all joy, all emotion, all purpose, he wishes only to be left in complete solitude. In the end, St. Peter chooses to fill the void with stoic acceptance of a life "without delight" (282). What he "let[s] go," that "something very precious" are his youthful illusions, what Reinhold Niebuhr called "the illusions of our national infancy— the illusion of our innocence, virtue, and omnipotence—the feeling that the American is born into a permanent and air-conditioned Eden."[55]

Once he becomes resigned to his current situation, St. Peter is once again able to feel "the ground under his feet" and believes that he knows where he is, that he can now "face with fortitude the Berengaria and the future" (283).

"In creating the image of the past, we create ourselves,"[56] wrote Robert Penn Warren. For Cather, the means to filling the vacuum left by the loss of youthful illusions lay in a re-visioning of the heroic pastoral and in the philosophical tenet echoed by Godfrey St. Peter, one that would inform her next three novels: "Art and religion (they are the same thing in the end, of course) have given man the only happiness he has ever had" (69).

In her short novel *My Mortal Enemy,* published between *The Professor's House* and *Death Comes for the Archbishop,* Cather not only further explores the connections between art and religion but also concedes the impossibility of escaping one's cultural heritage. Myra Henshawe's ideological heritage, like everyone's, has evolved from a predetermined enculturation—that is, it existed prior to her birth.[57] Escape from this earlier indoctrination seems virtually impossible. When Myra Henshawe tells Nellie Birdseye, "Yes, I broke with the Church when I broke with everything else and ran away with a German free-thinker; but I believe in holy words and holy rites all the same" (85), she demonstrates the difficulty, if not futility, in attempting to break from, for better or worse, "the stuff our forebears put into us" (82). She is equally unsuccessful at attempting to separate art from religion. Moreover, her elopement with Oswald Henshawe incites more than a break with the Church, for she also severs her ties with her wealthy uncle to whom she is the only living heir, rejecting, ostensibly for love, her eventual place in society among her "own kind" (75). Painfully ill and dying, Myra confronts, in bitterness, what she has given up, wishing that she still had "her circle" and "courtesy from people of gentle manners" (75). She acknowledges that she has become more like her uncle as she grows older, "can feel his savagery strengthen" (82) in her, that she carries within her own nature blood ties which she now believes she has betrayed.

Myra Henshawe returns to her Catholic heritage in her final days. She is fully aware that her earlier role as the romantic heroine who has rejected social position and wealth for love is at best a hollow sham. Thus Myra attempts to resurrect her earlier childhood religious teachings, which will allow her to die with dignity and aesthetic beauty. Critics generally disagree as to whether or not Myra's conversion is genuine.[58] But if Myra is selfish and self-centered to the end, she at least achieves an honest perception of her failures. Unlike Oswald who would insist they had always been happy, Myra refuses to make apologies for herself: "I am a greedy, selfish, worldly woman; I wanted success and a place in the world" (75), she tells Nellie. Yet even after Myra's death Oswald, like Niel Herbert, continues to hold on to his illusions, advising Nellie Birdseye to remember the earlier Myra, not as she was in California. In so doing, he denies the Myra who struggled to accept the truth of what she had made of her life. Like Jim Burden and Niel Herbert, Oswald Henshawe prefers the youthful vision, claiming that "nothing ever took that girl from me" (104).

Following *My Mortal Enemy*, Cather would continue to employ her pastoral/heroic visions in her fiction but in a new and different way. She would likewise continue what she had begun in *My Ántonia, The Lost Lady*, and *The Professor's House:* the exploration of the myth/historicity matrix. What had been the destructive hierarchical structures behind the U.S. expansionist policies in her plains novels, would, in her next two novels *Death Comes for the Archbishop* and *Shadows on the Rock*, be reconfigured as benevolent forms of power.

# 4

## *For Their Own Good*
### Cather's Pastoral Histories

> As I see it, the historical consciousness is not some-
> thing that is active in poems, novels, and plays only
> when a given and generally well-known historical
> event appears in the narrative, but a force or progress
> basic to many a writer's way of thinking, something
> implicit in his way of understanding and ordering
> our lives in time.
> —Richard Gray, *The Literature of Memory*

> In other words, in a primal way, in a gut way, the
> study of the past gives one a feeling for the structure
> of experience, for continuity, for establishing loca-
> tion on the shifting chart of being.
> —Robert Penn Warren, "The Use of the Past"

For more than two centuries the Southern literary imagination has been grounded in history. Like her ancestors, Cather too was deeply interested in the past, absorbing family histories from her father at an early age, listening to tales of the Civil War and the occupation from family members and friends. But her treatment of history within her fictional boundaries had been, until *Death Comes for the Archbishop*, primarily empirical. In writing *Archbishop*, however, Cather relied on numerous historical sources[1] and on the information she gathered from her five trips to the Southwest to enhance the credibility of her fictional world. Yet, as with any novel that employs historical fact, we must look at how this knowledge is represented in her text.

For all their historical facts, Cather preferred to call *Death Comes for*

*the Archbishop* "a narrative" (*WCW* 12) in "the style of legend," as in "the
Golden Legend . . . of the saints" (9), and *Shadows on the Rock* "a prose
composition . . . a series of pictures remembered rather than experienced" (15). Although she employed historical details in both novels,
Cather seems to have been aware of the responsibility involved when incorporating factual events and historical figures in her work. Always true
to her mythopoeic imagination, she did not consider either work to be
historical fiction. Moreover, Cather gives us a clue as to how she would
have us read the first of these two novels. In the Prologue of *Archbishop,*
the Spanish Cardinal María de Allande confesses to Father Ferrand that
his knowledge of America is "chiefly drawn from the romances of Fenimore Cooper" (11). When Father Ferrand gently corrects the Cardinal's
misconception regarding the Native Americans of the Southwest living
in wigwams, the Cardinal replies, "No matter, Father. I see your redskins
through Fenimore Cooper, and I like them so" (13). Cather seems to be
suggesting, first, that her book is by no means a historical romance and,
second, that she will attempt in her representation to rectify incorrect
assumptions about native populations. Cather, however, makes no pretense to accuracy in her reconstruction. For all her historical research
and interest in righting old wrongs, her responsibility was always to her
art.[2] Both *Death Comes for the Archbishop* and *Shadows on the Rock,* although they appear to place history and politics in the background while
concentrating on the lives of the characters, nevertheless possess a political agenda implicit in her use of the pastoral. As Lucinda MacKethan
notes, "the pastoralist of any age or environment envisions a particular
social structure which becomes a dramatic mechanism for making com-
parisons between real and ideal worlds, for distinguishing between the
artificial and the natural, for examining systems of values for any one of
a great variety of purposes, emotional and political as well as artistic."[3]
Biographical evidence certainly supports the emotional purpose underlying the writing of these books.[4] Moreover, Cather's own religious affiliation (formerly Baptist) had changed in 1922 when she joined the Grace
Episcopal Church in Red Cloud. And, as became evident in *The Professor's House,* she had begun to view religion and art as evolving from
the same spiritual source. Thus, *Archbishop* explores the diverse spiritual
mysteries that are a part of all human experience. But Cather—always

interested in power constructs and in order—also began to examine social structures based on benevolent hierarchical systems.

The dominant mode of pastoral, then, in both *Archbishop* and *Shadows*, is what Harry Shaw calls "history as pastoral,"[5] a variation particularly conducive to supporting a political perspective. Concomitant with this mode is an implied ideological vision for the future. For Cather, this vision embraced a hierarchical paradigm and the resurrection of Old World values, a legacy of her Southern heritage. Moreover, her employment of the pastoral in both of these novels further links her work to Southern pastoral literature of the postbellum era as well as to the philosophy of the Southern Agrarians in its judgment of present social conditions by "an earlier and purer set of standards."[6]

Cather was not alone in her desire to see these Old World values reestablished. In 1925, the year she conceived of the idea for *Archbishop*, a group of four Southern writers, formerly identified with the Fugitive movement at Vanderbilt, had begun to turn their attention to social and cultural concerns of the South with the hope of altering its industrial course. Because Cather's use of the pastoral is linked to the Southern literary imagination, a closer examination of the philosophical tenets of the Southern Agrarians yields further evidence that Cather's sensibility was unquestionably Southern. Although she had not lived in the South for over four decades, her philosophical and cultural outlook appears to have evolved along the same path as many of the writers affiliated with the Agrarian movement.

The Agrarians' visions for the future are posited in *I'll Take My Stand*.[7] The philosophies of John Crowe Ransom, Allen Tate, and to some extent, Donald Davidson often parallel Cather's in their anti-industrialism and anti-materialism, as well as in their pastoral vision, religious sensibility, and Old World viewpoint.[8] Not all of the Southern Agrarians, of course, were in full agreement on the issues, but all believed that the preservation of the Southern way of life, in spite of American industrial progress, was vital to their cause. Their introductory "Statement of Principles" summarizes the distinction between these two factions (the Southern way of life and American industrialization) as "Agrarian *versus* Industrial."[9] But the underlying forces propelling the movement went far beyond the need to preserve the traditional rural way of life once associated with the antebellum South. Motivated by a deep-seated desire to reconstruct their historical heritage, to resurrect the best of their culture, to distinguish the South as unique and separate from the materialistic, consumer-oriented direction of the rest of the nation, and to redefine its artistic and spiritual roots, the Southern Agrarians, like Cather, looked to the past in an attempt to discover their future. For Davidson, this position meant that Southerners had to slam the door on progress while retaining their "spiritual values against the fiery gnawing of industrialism." [10]

Willa Cather's own despair and disillusionment over the modern industrial age, with its empty materialistic values, were evident even prior to her writing *A Lost Lady* and *The Professor's House*. In her 1922 Pulitzer Prize–winning novel *One of Ours*,[11] protagonist Claude Wheeler, who is unable to adjust to a life of "mechanical toys," wonders why his father, a rich farmer, thinks nothing of spending money on new cars and farm machinery but considers going out to dinner an extravagance. Claude is deeply aware of his family's preoccupation with financial success and of the changing face of his town: "With prosperity came a kind of callousness; everybody wanted to destroy the old things they used to take pride in. The orchards, which had been nursed and tended so carefully twenty years ago, were now left to die of neglect. It was less trouble to run into town in an automobile and buy fruit than it was to raise it" (88–89). Even the people he has known all his life have begun to change. Rather than preserving the old communal way of life, "now they were continually having lawsuits" (89).

These sentiments regarding industrialized America and its effects on the spiritual and cultural values of society, so similar to those of the Southern Agrarians, would inform Cather's next three novels: *A Lost Lady*, *The Professor's House*, and *My Mortal Enemy*. Moreover, the link to France and to Old World European culture, which is alluded to in *One of Ours* and later developed in *Archbishop* and *Shadows*, further associates her with the Agrarians. In many ways, Cather herself exemplifies John Crowe Ransom's "reconstructed but unregenerate" Southerner who, although out of fashion, "persists in his regard for a certain terrain, a certain history, and a certain inherited way of living."[12] While Ransom and Tate may have disagreed on the most influential European country to mold the Old South—for Ransom it was England, for Tate, France—

both men understood the spiritual and aesthetic values that had shaped the antebellum culture. "The South," wrote Ransom, "is unique on this continent for having defended a culture which was according to the European principles of culture; and the European principles had better look to the South if they are to be perpetuated in this country."[13]

With Americans in a constant state of frenzied flux, their eyes focused on materialistic progress, the aesthetic ways of the Old South were in danger of dying out with the next generation. "You Americans are always looking for something outside yourselves to warm you up," Ernest tells Claude Wheeler in *One of Ours*. "In old countries, where not very much can happen to us, we know that,—and we learn to make the most of little things" (48). For the Agrarians and for Willa Cather, those "little things" were reflected in the way a person chose to live his or her life. In the antebellum South that choice included "the social arts of dress, conversation, manners, the table, the hunt, politics, oratory, the pulpit," what Ransom calls "the arts of living" and "community arts."[14] All of Cather's books, to some degree, illustrate this sentiment. How a human being chooses to live is a reflection of his artistic sensibility. Once in France, in the midst of war, Claude Wheeler discovers this simple truth through his friendship with David Gerhardt, a man of refined tastes from an old European family. In *Archbishop*, both Latour and Vaillant maintain an orderly and refined existence in the middle of a "savage country." In *Shadows*, Cécile Auclair turns the simple everyday tasks of maintaining a household into an art form, an aesthetically spiritual existence that has little to do with her small cramped home or with the acquisition of possessions but much to do with a desire for order and security.

Like Cather, who felt an affinity not only with the Catholic Church[15] but even more specifically with the spiritual dimensions of France, Allen Tate was, as he wrote to Davidson, "more and more heading towards Catholicism" having "reached a condition of the spirit where no further compromise is possible."[16] Tate believed the Old South closely resembled France in its religious and social sensibility. The postbellum South, he suggested, continued to "cling blindly to forms of European feeling and conduct that were crushed by the French Revolution and that, in England at any rate, are barely memories."[17] Six years earlier, prior to the publication of *I'll Take My Stand*, Tate was already aware of the potential for reestablishing a prototype of the old Europe in the American South, a Europe that no longer existed following World War I. In a letter to Davidson he wrote: "Philosophically we must go the whole hog of reaction, and base our movement less upon the actual old South than upon its prototype—the historical, social, and religious scheme of Europe. We must be the last Europeans—there being no Europeans in Europe at present."[18] Cather, too, was aware of the vast changes that had begun to take place in Europe following the war, as is evident in her short story "The Old Beauty." Yet both Tate and Cather envisioned a similar prototype based on early European history, a hierarchical paradigm that linked art and religion.

Just as many of the Southern writers of the 1920s and 1930s began to reconstruct the best of their historical past with a hope of creating a better future, Cather began to explore what she saw as the positive impact of early European culture in the New World. In so doing, she retained her pastoral vision but altered her earlier perception of the heroic. She replaced her heroic pioneer conquerors with men of the cloth, men who similarly faced hostility and potential death in a strange country but were sustained by their faith.

By 1926 she had made five trips to the Southwest and had become familiar with its history and culture. Through her extensive research, Cather must have become acutely aware of the violent conquest and exploitation inflicted on the indigenous peoples of the area. Even the pueblo of Ácoma, "Enchanted Mesa," symbol of safety and security, we learn, "had never been taken by a foe but once,—by Spaniards in armour" (96–97). *Death Comes for the Archbishop* addresses historical issues that are barely alluded to in *The Professor's House,* although St. Peter's histories are about the Spanish conquerors. Thus we are now told the Spaniards had treated the natives badly (54). Coronado and his men are no longer heroic explorers but bearers of contagious diseases, looters and spoilers. Upon leaving the Pecos village, they take slaves and concubines with them, and ultimately decimate a once thriving civilization of six thousand, reducing its population to a pitiful one hundred (123–24).[19] But while she accurately portrays the Native Americans' demise, Cather is particularly harsh in her portrayal of both the Spaniards and the Mexicans, many of whom, like Padre Martinez and Padre Lucero, are based on historical figures. As early as the prologue, we are told that the Spanish Cardinal María de Allande's eyes "showed a glint of yellow" (8–9). Similarly, Padre Martinez, a Mexican, has "brilliant yellow eyes" (141) and is told by Father Lucero, who sees Martinez in his deathbed vision, to "eat [his] tail." The images, of course, suggest Satan. Indeed, Padre Martinez is depicted as a lascivious womanizer, a glutton, and a political agitator. Father Lucero is portrayed as a grasping, greedy man, who hordes his money. Similarly, the aristocratic Manuel Chavez, we learn, had spent his boyhood "hunting Navajos" as "a form of sport . . . for spoil and adventure" (184).

These are the aristocratic and spiritual leaders of what Cather calls "The Old Order," a phrase she also chooses as the title of the first chapter of Book Five. Unlike her implicit allusions to The Old Order (the Forresters) and The New Order (Ivy Peters) in A Lost Lady, which symbolically parallel the antebellum and postbellum industrialized South, Cather seems to be suggesting an alternative way of looking at these terms. In Archbishop, The Old Order (the Hispanic/Mexican clergy) is portrayed as corrupt. The New Order, the French civilizing forces of the Church, offers not industrialization but rather hope and redemption, much in the same way that Tate perceived the redemptive possibilities in establishing an Old World prototype in the American South.

Cather's fictional world takes on the philosophical ideals later put forth by Tate in a letter to Davidson from Paris in which he describes his paradigm for a new South, one based on "a complete social, philosophical, literary, economic, and religious system" that would "inevitably draw upon [their Southern] heritage." Even so, this heritage, according to Tate, "should be valued, not in what it actually performed, but in its possible perfection."[20] Cather's New Order, like Tate's, would not make the mistakes of the past but would learn from history, as is evident when, on his deathbed, Bishop Latour reflects on having lived "to see two great wrongs righted . . . the end of black slavery . . . and the Navajos restored to their own country" (292), thus linking the two experiences, that of the South and the Southwest.[21] The Bishop's sentiments seem to be Cather's as well. By acknowledging the corruption of both histories and linking them to European roots, Cather universalizes the American experience, while simultaneously establishing her benevolent and artistic vision for a New Order.

In her quest for order and civilizing forces, Cather once again sets out to merge two seemingly opposing forces: the doctrines of the Catholic Church and the ancient spiritual traditions of the indigenous peoples. Her latest heroic figures may not brandish swords or conquer through fear and bloodshed,[22] but rather their objective is ecumenical preemption. Instead of deadly weapons, Cather's new heroes offer education and spiritual guidance. Instead of conquering the physical body, their objective is to win over the mind and soul. They are the men of her New Order, leaders who would draw upon their religious training and the best of their European heritage to create, through benevolent means, a spiritual and artistic community. Her heroes are now French missionaries, men "to whom order is necessary—as dear as life" (*DCA* 8), men such as Bishop Jean Marie Latour, a cultured and gentle upper-class man of refined tastes.

Just as Carlyle, whom Cather deeply admired, looked to Abbot Samson, a medieval monk who had established order in his monasteries during the Middle Ages,[23] and to the earlier feudal barons for inspiration,[24] Cather likewise sought a benevolent hierarchy to bring order and peace, in Carlyle's words, to those whose "souls are driven nigh mad."[25]

Unlike Jim Burden and Niel Herbert, who have been brought West without their consent, Latour and his companion Father Vaillant are exiles by choice. They have elected to come to this "savage country" (50), this "dark continent" (21), for the purpose of saving souls and establishing order. "Our Spanish fathers made good martyrs but the French Jesuits accomplish more," Cardinal de Allande tells Father Ferrand. "They are the great organizers . . . the Germans classify, but the French arrange!" (9). To further establish the need for order, Cather describes the Southwest landscape that awaits Latour as a barren wilderness. The mesa has the "appearance of great antiquity" and "incompleteness" (95). The narrator's statement that the "country was still waiting to be made into a landscape" (95) echoes Jim Burden's first impressions of the Nebraska plains. This "dark continent" implicitly awaits the organizing forces of the Church.

The Catholic clergy create gardens, metaphorically bringing symmetrical beauty to the chaos of the barren landscape. Not all of these gardens signify a New Eden, an imposed spiritual order. They do, however, frequently signify the spiritual condition of the gardener. Latour enters Father de Baca's house by way of his garden, a space filled with indigenous plants, domesticated cactus plants, and wicker cages containing colorful parrots, whose feathers the Indians prize. Father de Baca's garden is designed to welcome and please his parishioners. Conversely, Friar Baltazar's garden, filled with magnificent peach trees, must be watered every night by the native women of his parish. A greedy man, he takes the best of the corn, beans, and squashes from the Indians, while sharing nothing of his own. He makes long journeys "in behalf of his mission and his garden," once making a journey of several days to Oraibi to procure "their best peach seeds" (104). His garden is "like a little kingdom" (106), which he selfishly keeps for himself. His denouement, one he has brought upon himself when he inadvertently kills a young servant boy out of anger (one might say he has become the snake in his own garden), is carried out by the very Indians whose spiritual care was supposed to have been his primary concern. Disgusted with the Friar's behavior, they throw him off the most dangerous precipice of their high rock dwelling.

By contrast, Archbishop Latour's garden serves as an apt metaphor for the growth of his diocese. His five bulbs, brought from France (206), like the biblical five loaves, have miraculously multiplied, as have his parishioners. The cuttings from his apple and cherry trees "were already yielding fruit in many Mexican gardens" (201).

Recent scholars have been particularly critical of Cather's selective use of historical data, and at times, actual distortions, which raises the issue of the artist's obligations to history. Certainly there has been considerable controversy over Cather's harsh treatment of Padre Martinez, whose historical reputation—promoted predominantly through *Archbishop*—has suffered because of the author's omissions and alterations. Critics Ted J. Warner and Lance Larsen both address the methods by which Cather alters fact to enhance her artistic vision.[26] Although she uses details and specific episodes taken primarily from Howlett's biography of Machebeuf, Cather exaggerates Padre Martinez's lascivious lifestyle and his rebellious nature. As Larsen points out, she purposely omits Martinez's acts of community service because they would conflict with her portrait of a self-interested priest.[27] Cather's rebellious and at times heretical Martinez serves as the perfect foil for the serene, pious, deeply religious Bishop Latour.

Curiously, Cather elects to change the surnames of her two righteous priests while retaining Martinez's true identity. Warner suggests Cather changed the surnames of her French priests to conform to her artistic vision of them: Latour as "a tower of strength" and Vaillant as "valiant in the faith."[28] But by retaining the names not only of Martinez but also of all the Hispanic/Mexican priests, and portraying many of them with contempt, Cather has, as Warner suggests, in effect contributed to, if not launched, the "Martinez Myth,"[29] as well as effectively condemned the actual, that is, historically verifiable, Old Order.[30]

While the following statement may seem to privilege literature, that is, a fictional text, over other texts, let me suggest that Cather's rendering of Latour's personality is the key to how we should read and interpret the character of Padre Martinez. The Padre is revealed to us through Latour's perspective, not to be confused with Cather's. Moreover, Cather's portrait of her Bishop is, at times, also unflinching. She is well aware of his elitist shortcomings. She depicts Latour as a man of refined tastes, given to order and cleanliness, who harshly judges his more earthy antagonist: he finds "the food poor enough, despite the many cooks" (145), and although Martinez graciously tells Latour to consider his house as his own, the Bishop has no such desire: "the disorder was almost more than his fastidious taste could bear" (144). The Bishop shows none of the Christian charity toward Martinez that one would expect from a man of the cloth. In fact, Latour dislikes Martinez's "personality so much that he [can] scarcely look at him" (145).

Latour's elitism, his unfamiliarity with the Hispanic/Mexican culture, and his lack of a generous spirit when a situation is highly subjective reflect poorly on the Bishop. But his point of view is nevertheless consistent with the Catholic Church's official position, which would have found anything that Martinez did that had not been sanctioned by the Church as an act of heresy or rebellion, overshadowing his more noble qualities. Therefore Padre Martinez appears in the book as he would have appeared in the eyes of the ecclesiastical authority during this period of history, making Cather's rendition historically accurate for what it is intended to represent. *Death Comes for the Archbishop* is, after all, among other things, as Cather herself noted, "the story of the Catholic Church in that Country [the Southwest]" (*WCW* 5).

The conflict, however, is not only between Latour and Martinez but also between European and Native American cultures. Padre Martinez warns Latour: "The Church the Franciscan Fathers planted here was cut off; this is the second growth, and is indigenous. Our people are the most devout left in the world. If you blast their faith by European formalities, they will become infidels and profligates" (147). The Old Order, the established Hispanic/Mexican clergy, it seems, still has much to teach the New Order (just as Tate suggested the New South had much to learn from the best of its own past). "The dark things forbidden by your Church are a part of Indian religion. You cannot introduce French fashions here" (148), Martinez tells Latour, warning him not "to interfere with the secret dances of the Indians" and advising him "to study our native traditions before [he] begins his reforms" (148).

John Murphy correctly points out that Padre Martinez is right and that he likewise represents Cather's own viewpoint,[31] one that had grown in sympathy with the displacement of Native populations. As Murphy notes, Martinez's position is reinforced further by Kit Carson's Mexican wife who hopes Father Latour will not attempt to "put a stop to the extravagances of the Penitential Brotherhood" (155).[32] "The old people have need of their customs" (155), she tells him.

Thus the Church functions as a powerful force for change, one that could replace the indigenous cultures with the Western European tradition. Like the pioneer aristocracy that built railroads, changing the face of the West, Bishop Latour's obsession is to build a simple but beautiful cathedral, which in its way will also bring change. Similarly, Father Vaillant purchases massive tracks of land for the Church in Colorado. The building of new structures and acquisition of land continue; only the builders and acquisitors have changed, and inevitably, change brings conflict.

Indeed, the book is rife with the clashes of different cultures: American, Hispanic/Mexican, French, and Native American, all vying for power, and there is a fifth player on the field, one that could assimilate all of the others: the Church. The Church has the power to bring art and spirituality to people of all cultures, classes, and races, to establish a unifying whole, an alternative paradigm to the sometimes dehumanizing effects of the modern industrial age. Such a world would be composed of grace and beauty, lush gardens and edifices that are works of art, based on French models (the Bishop's garden blooms from bulbs brought from France; his Cathedral is modeled after the Midi Romanesque of his own country). Even Dona Isabella, a Southerner born in Kentucky and raised in Louisiana, who has been educated in a French convent, has "done much to Europeanize her husband," (176) Antonio Olivares. Cather's philosophical paradigm, like Tate's, once again connects the French culture to the Old South, in this case through Dona Isabella.

But Cather offers us yet another view of art and spirituality through the folk art and religious wooden statues of the Native Americans and Mexicans and through the stories surrounding their secret ceremonies. Father Vaillant openly embraces the Native Americans and Mexicans, although he has little patience for Padre Martinez. Concerned that Father Latour has called him back to Santa Fe permanently, Vaillant contends, " 'down there it is work for the heart, for a particular sympathy, and none of our new priests understand those poor natures as I do. I have almost become a Mexican! I have learned to like *chili colorado* and mutton fat. Their foolish ways no longer offend me, their very faults are dear to me. I am *their man!* " (208). Both men operate on different levels, however, and Latour, aware not only of the religious responsibility of his position but also of the cultural, chooses to remain more aloof. The ancient mysteries of the Native Americans threaten his sense of order. When his guide Jacinto leads him to a sacred cavern to seek shelter from a blizzard, Latour becomes deeply disturbed by the experience. "I feel ill here already" (128), he tells the guide. "[O]ne of the oldest voices of the earth," the water rushing below "in utter blackness under ribs of antediluvian rock," a sound of "majesty and power" (130), overwhelms him. "It is terrible" (130), he tells Jacinto. Before he is able to sleep, he makes Jacinto "repeat a *Pater Noster* with him" (131).

Similarly, even though Latour works to help the Church build its ecumenical constituency, his attitude toward his parishioners is sometimes condescending. He often refers to his guide Jacinto as "boy," although the Indian is a twenty-six-year-old man with a wife and child. On their journey to Ácoma, the Bishop at first makes little attempt to understand what he calls "the Indian mind" (92), which suggests that he perceives Jacinto not as an individual so much as a representative of his race. Thus he seldom questions "Jacinto about his thoughts or beliefs," ostensibly because he doesn't "think it polite" (92). On the one hand we might view, as does John Murphy, Latour's position as sympathetic, an acceptance of those things he does not understand.[33] Because there is no way he can "transfer his own memories of European civilization" (92) to his guide's mind, he believes it would be unlikely Jacinto could ever share his own long, ancient heritage. On the other hand, unlike Father Vaillant, who is more open to the people of his parish, Latour does not really make an effort to understand Jacinto, any more than he attempts to comprehend Martinez's position or that of the other Hispanic clergy. Latour and Vaillant are intentionally juxtaposed opposites. Latour, as Vaillant recognizes, "would have been better placed in some part of the world where scholarship, a handsome person, and delicate perceptions all have their effect" (253–54).

Bishop Latour, however, like Thea Kronborg and Tom Outland, does desire to find a commutual connection between his culture and the Native Americans in his parish. A man of God, the Bishop strives to establish common ground between his religious beliefs and what he considers to be the mysteries of Indian spirituality. But in so doing, he, like Tom and Thea, inadvertently imposes his own belief system on the Other. He perceives the Canyon de Chelly to be a place where the Navajos believe their gods dwell, where they hold religious ceremonies. When Latour and his French architect visit the old cliff ruins, they see the sheep "grazing under the magnificent cottonwoods and drinking at the streams of sweet water; it was like an Indian Garden of Eden" (297). Just as Tom and Rodney name the Indian mummy "Mother Eve," the Bishop imposes his religious beliefs on the Other to establish a desired, yet nonetheless imagined, connection.[34] But though Bishop Latour will never be a man of the people like Father Vaillant, Cather suggests a unifying of the two cultures when, at the end of the novel, "the old Archbishop" sits wrapped "in his Indian blankets . . . looking at the open, golden face of his Cathedral" (271).

Yet Latour's attitude toward Jacinto, Sada, and his other less fortunate parishioners is thoroughly consistent with the pastoral tradition, which assumes it is the duty of the powerful and wealthy to protect the weak and the poor,[35] an ideological assumption that is equally prevalent in *Shadows on the Rock*. Thus Latour believes in the Church's power "to make these poor Mexicans 'good Americans' . . . for the people's good; [because] there is no other way in which they can better their condition" (36).

Like its predecessor, *Shadows* seeks to establish a secure and orderly world through implicit hierarchical power structures in the form of a pastoral ideal.[36] Cather envisioned *Shadows* as "a series of pictures" (*WCW* 15). With the ideal of domestic order and tradition as a central focus in the novel, it certainly fits the most fundamental definition of pastoral: "a series of little pictures, or 'eidyllion,' with a dream or ideal at its heart."[37] Moreover, through the character of Cécile, it is possible to make a strong case for Renato Poggioli's "pastoral of innocence," acknowledging the "psychological root of the pastoral [as] a double longing after innocence and happiness, to be recovered not through conversion or regeneration, but merely through a retreat."[38] Thus "the natural outcome of the pastoral of innocence is the family situation, or the domestic idyll."[39]

Written during a time of intense stress for Cather, *Shadows* exemplifies the author's deep desire for order and stability. As Merrill Maguire Skaggs notes, "One impulse behind *Shadows on the Rock* . . . is as old as the species: to create the image of a safe place in which to live, or to find an image of life that one might associate with safety."[40] The fictional world Cather creates moves beyond the structured and orderly life Latour leads within his ecclesiastical family to envision an idealized community, one based securely on Old World spiritual and aesthetic values.

Willa Cather's state of mind during the writing of *Shadows* has been well documented by her biographers. We know it was a time filled with tragic loss and suffering: the death of her father, followed by her mother's paralyzing stroke, the loss of her apartment at 5 Bank Street, and the news of Isabelle McClung's illness. Following her father's death, and the loss of her apartment, Cather and her long-time companion Edith Lewis headed for Grand Manan Island where Cather had a small summer cottage. On the way they stopped in Quebec. According to Edith Lewis, Cather was "overwhelmed by the flood of memory, recognition, surmise it called up; by the sense of its extraordinarily French character, isolated and kept intact through hundreds of years, as if by a miracle, on this great unfrench continent."[41] Cather's description of *Shadows* as "pictures remembered rather than experienced; a kind of thinking, a mental complexion inherited, left over from the past" (*WCW* 15) suggests a connection between the Old World values of France (also, by extension, Quebec), and Cather's early childhood world, a Southern heritage based on similar values. As previously noted, historical sociologist Robert

A. Nisbet defines these Old World values as "hierarchy, community, tradition, authority, and the sacred sense of life."[42]

Cather often spoke of her father during the summer she began work on *Shadows*, following his death. Edith Lewis tells us that Cather's "mind often went back to his gentle protectiveness and kindness, the trusting relationship between them, in the old days in Virginia."[43] If Cather's memories of her father, a gentleman of the Old South (the prototype for the character of Euclide Auclair), took her back to these early recollections, it seems evident such memories would also have triggered a longing for the old ways and traditions, a need to connect, as did her character Myra Henshawe, to the heritage of her ancestors. Despite her earlier rejection of her Southern background, this same heritage now offered domestic rituals, order, tradition, and religious affiliation, all of which helped to maintain a stable environment. In a time of rapidly shifting change and personal tragedy, Cather was drawn to this order and domestic stability. They inform the very foundation of her prototype for New France. Moreover, she transposes her own traditional Southern values, which correspond with those of the Old World, to the small seventeenth-century community of Quebec. She creates a secure world—set apart from the greed and corruption of the Old World aristocracy—arcadian in its orderly simplicity and mythical in its religious adherence to art and ritual.

Cather's class consciousness, as we have seen, was instrumental in embellishing the pastoral with hierarchical structures, making them a condition of peace and stability. In *Some Versions of Pastoral*, William Empson reminds us how admiration for the "heroic-pastoral" can often be ironically distorted into an approval of aristocracy.[44] Cather's Canadian aristocrats are, for the most part, presented as powerful, yet wise and benevolent. Paternal and protective, they reside in the Upper Town, overlooking the shops and houses below, fulfilling their pastoral roles as guardians of those less fortunate. Count Frontenac represents dominion over the State and Bishop Laval, the ecclesiastical hierarchy.

Both the secular and nonsecular hierarchical dimensions are intended to function for the good of the community. The Count, Euclide Auclair's patron, is a paternal figure, ostensibly with Euclide's and Cécile's best interests at heart. Bishop Laval is a nurturing, almost maternal presence, who bathes little Jacques's feet and offers him food and drink. Cather has intentionally made these larger-than-life historical presences conducive to her vision of New France, a place seemingly exempt from the corruption of the Old World while still maintaining the best of the original cultural values. To further depict New France as an ideal society embracing the revered Old World values, she perpetuates the myth of the New World as a place of rebirth and renewal by contrasting it to the old France, which has lost these values and is governed by a corrupt, petty, and vindictive aristocracy, as is represented in the Church by the spoiled Bishop de Saint-Vallier, himself an aristocrat.

Still, while the benevolent nobility and ecclesiastical hierarchy watch over their charges from the Upper Town, we are reminded that "[n]ot one building on the rock was on the same level with any other,—" (5). In this society, each member knows and accepts his place. Euclide Auclair lives "under the Count's shadow. The Count [is] the reason for nearly everything he [does],—for his being here at all" (260).

Daily the Lower Town goes about its business of merchandising, trading, and prostitution. Both the lower and middle classes enjoy the kind, watchful concern of those in the Upper Town, and by extension, those secure in their bourgeois roles watch over those in the lower classes whom they view as less fortunate. Watching over the "less fortunate," aside from its pastoral and Carlylian allusions ("just subordination; noble loyalty in return for noble guidance"),[45] also has its direct correlation in the tradition of noblesse oblige: Cécile desires to purchase new shoes for little Jacques; she prepares old Blinker a hot meal each evening as her mother before her had done (just as Victoria Templeton in "Old Mrs. Harris" gives dimes to the Maude children, and Alexandra Bergson in O Pioneers! takes in old Ivar).

To understand further Cécile's position, we must take into consideration Cather's ambiguous relationship with her own mother and the stress she was coping with following her mother's stroke. Having rejected for so many years the domestic world of her mother, Cather now sought its safety. As Virginia Cather lay paralyzed in a Pasadena nursing home, Cather created the memorable scene between Cécile and her dying mother Madame Auclair, who passes on the secrets of maintaining an orderly household. "Without order our lives would be disgusting, like those of the poor savages," she tells Cécile. "At home, in France, we have learned to do all these things in the best way, and we are conscientious, and that is why we are called the most civilized people in Europe and other nations envy us" (24–25). What Madame Auclair wishes to leave with her daughter is that intangible "feeling about life that had come down to her through so many centuries and that she had brought with her across the wastes of obliterating, brutal ocean. The sense of 'our way,' " (25)—by which she means a preservation of cultural and domestic values. At the same time, Madame Auclair's assumptions regarding the indigenous natives of Canada are also being handed down to her daughter along with her instructions on running a civilized household, as were many of the Southern attitudes and prejudices inadvertently passed along to Cather by her own mother.

Madame Auclair envisions that after her death life will go on in the same orderly fashion, remaining unchanged "in this room with its dear (and to her, beautiful) objects; that the proprieties would be observed, all the little shades of feeling which make the common fine" (25). Madame Auclair's sensibilities call to mind Niel Herbert's feelings for the Forrester home, remind us, too, of what Myra Henshawe missed the most in her final days, and ultimately echo Cather's own aesthetic ideal. We are reminded, again, how Virginia Cather must have struggled to keep a sense of "our way"—those rigid proprieties young Willa once rebelled against—alive on the desolate prairie.

Why, then, does Cather choose New France as a prototype for this ideal social structure rather than set her story in the early South, particularly in view of her promise to her father that she would someday write a book about Virginia?[46] In Shadows on the Rock, Cather seems to have found a way of indirectly reuniting herself with her Virginia childhood through the same Old World European cultural roots that had eventually evolved into the antebellum society of the Old South. By setting her book in Canada, she was able to bypass the issue of slavery (the paradox that plagued many Southern writers, the conflict that arose when they attempted to incorporate chattel slavery with a pastoral vision of the Old South), while still preserving the Old World connection. Cather's indifference to her Southern heritage suggests that she may have been uncomfortable placing her hierarchical prototype for an idealized stable society in the South, concerned that her vision would not be acceptable to a postbellum world that would associate any Southern hierarchical system with the plantation aristocracy and chattel slavery, although Cather herself did not condone slavery. Still, the remaining parallels between the two cultures made her choice of New France compatible with her need to explore her early childhood values and hierarchical structures and to question implicitly whether these values and systems might be applied to present-day America.

In creating her pastoral world of innocence, her idealized community, Cather selected, as she did in *Death Comes for the Archbishop*, those historical facts that supported her ideological paradigm. In *Shadows*, as in her previous novel, Cather's facts are chosen to support a vision of a past that idealizes what appear on the surface to be symbiotic relationships but in actuality mask the more insidious issues of control and power.

While it is true Cather relied heavily on historian Francis Parkman's volumes of *France and England in North America*,[47] among other sources, to create an accurate portrait of life in late seventeenth-century Quebec, and while the background details are realistically depicted, she frequently used her poetic license to reinforce her vision of a small, harmonious, benevolent community. As Wilbur Jacobs has noted, Count Frontenac "was in fact one of the most arrogant, tempestuous, and brutal of French leaders, noted for permitting the torment and burning of Indian captives."[48] Although perhaps not as bloodthirsty as some of his counterparts, he was nevertheless far from the good-natured, "amiable and benign" protector Cécile and her father would have us believe.[49] Cather does hint, however, that some of the other characters fear Frontenac, which suggests we are experiencing the benevolent Frontenac from primarily Cécile's and Euclide's points of view, just as we are asked to see Martinez through Latour's eyes.

To privilege the historical reality, of course, would have undermined Cather's pastoral vision, a mythical world where the early morning church bell lends "a peculiar sense of security" and begins an "orderly procession of activities" that hold "life together on the rock" (105), where "kindly lights" burn in the windows of "neighbours' houses" (104) and where aristocratic patrons restore "peace and order" by chastising Indians and securing "the safety of trade" (238). Although pain and suffering are not excluded from the rock, any more than they are from Arcadia, they are nevertheless made endurable because of the inhabitants' strict adherence to the Old World values. Cather's Quebec is a world of myth and miracle, and above all, innocence, a "Kebec," Count Frontenac tells Auclair, "as near heaven as any place" (242).

In order to enhance her vision of the security and continuity of life on the rock, Cather creates a negative juxtaposition, a chaotic world represented by the forests beyond the city: "That was the dead, sealed world of the vegetable kingdom, an unchartered continent choked with interlocking trees, living, dead, half-dead, their roots in bogs and swamps, strangling each other in a slow agony that had lasted for centuries" (6–7). The forest is also home to "the savages" who pose a constant threat to the ordered world nestled securely on the rock. But what Cather neglects to share with us is that a confederation government established by the allegedly "brutal" Huron-Iroquois was, in fact, a civilized structure, and that their development of "a system of subsistence farming . . . rivaled the old nation-states of Europe."[50] Cather's mythopoeic version, of course, serves as a powerful metaphor for the destructive outside forces that would overpower the fragile arcadian world of New France, had the people of Quebec not adhered religiously to their Old World traditions. But at the same time, according to Jacobs, it also serves as a grave injustice to the Huron-Iroquois nation.[51] Considering Cather's earlier sympathetic treatment of Native Americans in *Archbishop*, however, I would like to suggest that her rendering of the Hurons in *Shadows* was intended to replicate the perceptions of the seventeenth-century citizens of Quebec who would have feared any outside force that threatened their fragile security. A more sympathetic depiction of the seventeenth-century attitudes toward the Hurons would have been historically inaccurate.

It is evident that Cather, even while incorporating historical fact, continued to mythologize much of her material to sustain her pastoral vision within her fictional worlds. But she had come too far in her exploration of the past and in her own psychological connection to it to abandon the historical dimension. For just as she had become disillusioned with the modern industrial age, she grew equally discouraged with modern Europe. France was now almost as far from the Old World of the Middle Ages, an age in which Cather had longed to live,[52] as the industrialized United States. Only Quebec had remained unchanged, a timeless vision of the past.

In *My Mortal Enemy* Myra Henshawe mourned the severing of her earlier ancestral roots. But in *Shadows on the Rock*, those in exile, such as Euclide Auclair, have learned to survive through the support of family, the patronage of the Count, and connection to the community and to the Church. Where Jim Burden, Niel Herbert, Godfrey St. Peter, and Myra Henshawe had been disconnected, Cather's characters in *Shadows* share a history, are part of the great web. Cécile and her father not only are part of the New France community but also are firmly tied to their ancestral past through family connections back in the Old World.

After years of dismissing her Southern roots, it was now time for Cather to reconnect to her own historical past. During the 1920s and 1930s, Southern writers who had been disengaged from their cultural past had already begun a kind of historical restoration, "a reconstruction ... of memory and history."[53] Seven years after the publication of *Shadows on the Rock*, Cather would reclaim "memory and history" and begin her own reconstruction of her ancestral past in her last novel *Sapphira and the Slave Girl*.[54] She would continue to examine hierarchical power structures and to explore thematic issues of possession and control, but this time she would fulfill her father's wish and situate her novel in Virginia. Cather chose to set her book in the pastoral plantation world of the antebellum South where, as did many of her Southern contemporaries, she would not only confront but also attempt to understand the paradox of the edenic vision in the pastoral "garden of the chattel."[55]

# 5

## *History and Memory*
### Cather's Garden of the Chattel

> I had the sense of coming home to myself, and of
> having found out what a little circle man's experi-
> ence is.
>
> —from *My Ántonia*

> Even if the Southerner prays to feel different, he may
> still feel that to change his attitude would be a
> treachery—to that City of the Soul which the histori-
> cal Confederacy became, to blood spilled in hopeless
> valor, to the dead fathers, and even to the self. He is
> trapped in history.
>
> —Robert Penn Warren, *The Legacy of the Civil War*

*I*n the 1930s when the national literary conscience was turning to social issues, Southern writers, conversely, looked not to present un-
rest for their subject but chose instead to seek meaning and order
in their own unique past. With Faulkner, Wolfe, Warren, Tate, and others, the first phase of the Southern Literary Renaissance was born.[1] These
writers focused on history with the hope of better understanding their
place in the present.[2] During this time, as Lewis P. Simpson points out,
"Southern writing records an attempted reconstruction of the meaning
of the past by the literary mind: a struggle to arrest the disintegration of
memory and history."[3] Called romantics, mythmakers, and escapists by
the social critics of the era, they nonetheless persevered in their literary
quest, a search for a more personal historical truth, or as Robert Penn
Warren called it, "a mode of memory . . . an actuality as remembered,"[4]
that would give meaning to past events.

Cather, too, came under attack by critics who interpreted her interest in the past as a means of escape from the present. In a 1933 essay, Granville Hicks accused Cather of having "never once tried to see contemporary life as it is."[5] But Hicks, like many of the critics in both the North and South during that time, misinterpreted the conflation of past and present in the Southern literature of the 1930s and 1940s.[6] The issues were far more complex than an inability to face present reality. Moreover, many Southern writers who had only begun to explore their own history felt inadequate to the task of tackling the injustices of a modern industrial society, not the least of which was the exploitation of the labor forces, in some ways reminiscent of the South's former treatment of the black race.

During the years when Faulkner worked on *The Hamlet,* when Warren was writing his first novel *Night Riders,* and Welty was creating the short stories that would later appear in her first collection *A Curtain of Green and Other Stories,* Cather returned to her ancestral past for the subject of what would be her last published novel. Although her own Virginia childhood experiences had taken place during Reconstruction, she nevertheless elected to set her novel in the antebellum South. Her choice of place (Back Creek) and time (1856) allowed her to explore that period in history—so deeply connected to her own heritage—from a distance of several decades, and also allowed her a critical and ironic perspective. As Richard Weaver notes, "Southern literature became mature when it first became capable of irony."[7] Cather's particular brand of irony in *Sapphira* was aimed at undermining her readers' assumptions about the plantation novel and their preconceived ideas of the Old South.[8]

In *Death Comes for the Archbishop* and *Shadows on the Rock,* Cather not only examined benevolent hierarchical constructs but also further explored the dynamics of the conflation of history and myth in a fictional context. In her final novel she undertook a difficult personal challenge: confronting through memory the family history she had sought to ignore for so many years.

Cather's decision to base her final novel in Back Creek, Virginia, rather than in another Southern state or another part of Virginia suggests her need to examine the more personal familial dimensions that might possibly illuminate her own connection to the past. Her choice of setting—the antebellum period prior to the Civil War—was the outcome

of a natural progression begun as early as *O Pioneers!*, in which she explored hierarchical paradigms within pastoral constructs, a motif that
also incorporated her thematic concerns of order, control, and possession. Always intrigued by opposites and reversals and having previously
established a benign hierarchical system in *Shadows on the Rock*, Cather
now sought to understand the dark underside of such a system. By
choosing the pre–Civil War South in which to examine abusive power
structures, she cast her lot with those Southern writers who were likewise confronting their own historical past.

With the deaths of her parents, Cather's motivation for writing *Sapphira* appears to have been, in part, a desire to understand what influence, if any, being born a Southerner and raised in exile by a Southern
family had on her historical memory and cultural assumptions. We
know that personal memory was a compelling force behind the book, for
as Cather wrote to Dorothy Canfield Fisher, the writing of *Sapphira* began with the recollection of Negro voices.[9] Furthermore, in her letters to
Viola Roseboro, Cather confessed that her book might even be considered nonfiction since so many of the family and neighborhood stories
formed its foundation.[10] Cather's story is a composite of memory and
history, of family stories told and retold, and as is evident from the epilogue, of memorable people she knew in her childhood, of colors,
smells, tastes, and sights, all of which were connected to her earliest recollections. Not surprisingly, the original manuscript was considerably
longer than the final version. Starting the book with the intention of re-
cording the "complete history of manners and customs of the valley,"
she later found herself discarding a "good six pounds" of material that
she felt was not essential to her story (*WCP* 136). What remained, however, was a finely tuned study of the negative effects of the institution of
slavery on the minds both of slaveholders and of those living within the
system, as well as the corrosive impact on the moral, spiritual, and artistic sensibility.

As early as 1931, while on Grand Manan (around the time of her
mother's death), Cather began to explore the Southern dimensions and
cultural dynamics at work in her own family in the highly autobiographical short story "Old Mrs. Harris." In *Sapphira and the Slave Girl*
Cather would continue what she had begun in "Old Mrs. Harris": an
examination of the customs and manners that were a part of her heri-

tage. Moreover, although the characters of Sapphira and Henry Colbert are ostensibly based on her maternal great-grandparents the Seiberts, many of the characteristics of Charles and Virginia Cather, as they appear in Mr. Templeton and his wife Victoria from "Old Mrs. Harris," are also evident in Sapphira and Henry, as David Stouck has pointed out, suggesting Cather's parents were also prototypes for the Colberts.[11] In many ways, the cultural beliefs of the main characters in Cather's last novel suggest her own "house divided": William Cather, his wife, and sons, Union sympathizers, and William Boak, his wife, and children, loyal Confederates. But *Sapphira and the Slave Girl* is far more than a book about customs and manners; it is also a study of the Old Order before the fall.

At the center is the pivotal force of Sapphira Dodderidge Colbert, around whom all else revolves. Merrill Maguire Skaggs has pointed out the complexity of Sapphira Colbert,[12] a fact frequently overlooked by other critics who merely find the character unlikable. But Sapphira is more than the embodiment of complex characteristics and opposing traits: kindness and treachery, strength and humility. She *is* the Old South in all its complexity and ambiguity as it moves toward its final years. Her nature is the paradox of the slave-owning culture. Through her, we can trace the insidious effects of the institution of slavery on the mind of the slave owner.

Proud, defiant, courageous, independent, stubborn, and equally cruel and kind, Sapphira, like Padre Martinez in *Death Comes for the Archbishop*, signifies the Old Order. With her swollen legs, her deformed feet and ankles, her crippled body, her wheelchair made by a coffin maker, and the sense of decay surrounding her, Sapphira resembles one of Faulkner's or O'Connor's grotesques. Just as Sapphira's stately long black dress hides her debilitating illness, the pretense of pastoral order belies the painful chaos within the system as the Old South lumbers toward its inevitable end.

On the surface the Mill House appears to be a stately but smaller version of Washington's Mount Vernon. With its upper and lower white-columned front porches, spanning the length of the house, its broad green lawns, sugar maples, locust trees, and numerous gardens, it is the quintessential pastoral plantation. The order, as in *Shadows on the Rock*, is maintained through daily domestic ritual. But unlike that in *Shadows*, the domestic order as well as the economic stability of the Mill Farm are intrinsically interwoven with chattel slavery. Behind the facade lies general disorder, a "helter-skelter" scattering of slave cabins (20). The grounds are littered with old tools and toys; wet shirts and dresses drip from clotheslines; chickens, turkeys, dogs, and cats chase about with the children. From the beginning Cather cautions us to look beneath the surface, behind the facade, beneath the polite exchanges between Sapphira and Henry, beyond the customs and manners to discern the truth about this deceptively pastoral setting.

Although pastoral motifs are present in the text, other fictional elements work against them, subverting the conventional assumptions. As Skaggs points out, Cather uses a series of reversals to undermine cultural stereotypes and expectations.[13] The antebellum and early postbellum novels, as Cather well knew, were often classic plantation pastorals. To employ this literary device seriously would have confirmed Granville Hicks's argument, as well as continued the perpetuation of the myth of the Old South readers had come to anticipate.[14] Furthermore, in so doing, she would have aligned herself with the antebellum and early postbellum writers who had attempted without success to incorporate chattel slavery into the pastoral myth. Not surprisingly, then, Cather alters the pastoral images associated with plantation life, while not wholly subverting them. The surrounding countryside, nature's domain outside the Mill House, remains idyllic, with descriptions of wood laurel, blossoming cherry trees, and Easter lilies untouched by the disorder and disharmony of the Mill House. The pastoral images are associated predominantly with the black servants: Till is the source of domestic order and serenity in the house, Jezebel has full dominion over the gardens, and many of Nancy's scenes take place in pastoral settings intended to signify her innocence and—as in the scene where Martin attempts to seduce Nancy who sits above him in a flowering cherry tree—the potential threat to that innocence.[15]

Conversely, Sapphira has lost contact with the land and with nature. Her sojourn to see the wild laurel in bloom is merely an opportunity to show herself to advantage in her glass-windowed carriage with the family crest on the door. Moreover, since "the contrast within Virgilian pastoral is," as previously noted, "between the pleasures of rural settlement and the threat of loss and eviction,"[16] we must consider that Cather has, from the beginning, already established Sapphira's position as being one of exile. Like Myra Henshawe, Sapphira has given up much of her former way of life, although she still visits friends and family. Yet, the humid, suffocating Back Creek woods to which she has come hardly affords her "the pleasures of a rural settlement," although she would never have admitted it to anyone.

Sapphira's exile, however, does not preclude the possibility of further loss. On the surface, the most immediate threat appears to be Nancy's inadvertent appropriation of Henry's affections. But upon closer examination, it becomes evident that Sapphira is struggling to preserve a way of life that she senses is in jeopardy. The domestic order and serenity on the surface belie an inner turmoil. For while chattel slavery is indeed a source of order to Sapphira, it is also a threat to the human mind and imagination.[17]

Thomas Jefferson, himself a slaveholder, paradoxically condemned the institution of chattel slavery in his *Notes on the State of Virginia*, but his concern was not with the effects of slavery on the slaves. Rather, foreseeing corruption within the moral fiber of the slaveholders, a breakdown in the customs and manners that upheld civility, his foreboding focused on the consequences of slavery on the minds of the slave owners.[18] For Jefferson, according to Simpson, "Slavery not only corrupts the young mind with the passion of command, it not only severs the connection between the mind of the master class and the soil, but it defies the very scrutiny of mind. Slavery destroys the very capacity for rational criticism. It implies the drastic dispossession of the pastoral vision of the plantation as a dominion of mind."[19] In *Sapphira*, the corruptive effects of slave ownership form the internal tensions within the characters' minds—that which is "felt upon the page" (*WCW* 41)—particularly with Sapphira, for we are rarely privy to her thoughts or motives.

"Those who labour in the earth are the chosen people of God,"[20] Jefferson proclaimed. The garden, then, becomes the domain of the slaves who till the soil, eventually dispossessing the master/owner who has severed his union not only with the land but, implicitly, with his Creator. Many of Cather's sympathetic characters are gardeners: we recall Alexandra leaning on her hoe in her garden, dreaming of the future; Ántonia plowing the fields and tending her orchards; Latour growing his garden from the seeds of his homeland; and Cécile carefully protecting the parsley from her tiny but sufficient garden. Sapphira, too, we are told, once worked side by side with her slave Jezebel to plant the shrubs, trees, and flowers that would bring grace and beauty to her pastoral Mill Farm. But once the initial planting is done, she turns the gardens over to Jezebel, giving her full charge. The Sapphira we encounter at the beginning of Cather's novel (although she deeply loves the land) no longer physically works the soil.

Sapphira also lacks a spiritual life. She is without a moral sense. Her appearance in the Episcopal Christ Church each Easter is merely affectation, for "no Dodderidge who ever sat in that pew showed her blood to better advantage" (29). Sapphira has "shallow blue eyes" (28), "a lively greenish blue, but with no depth" (15), eyes that have implicitly closed themselves off from critical inquiry. Acceptance of slavery as a natural condition and right of a privileged class defies "the very scrutiny of the mind." Sapphira is a product of an ideological construct that has incorporated chattel slavery into its economic survival, into its pastoral ideal (from a literary standpoint), and perhaps even more important, into its signification of self. Thus Sapphira will never question the system because her interpretation of self and her social status in life are defined in relation to it. Any critical discourse that led to moral inquiry would inevitably undermine the existing system.

The absence of any critical inquiry is further evident in Sapphira's lack of depth. She reads little,[21] and unlike most of Cather's protagonists, lacks any real aesthetic sensibility.[22] Any pretense to aristocratic behavior is to show herself to advantage among her less fortunate neighbors. Her imperious bearing and her careful attention to manners and tradition seem hollow and meaningless when contrasted with the loving details of the domestic rituals performed by her servants. Till's bathing of Sapphira's swollen ankles in hot water and massaging her legs—a scene reminiscent of Mandy's treatment of Old Mrs. Harris—has all the warmth and generosity of a truly gracious act.

Sapphira wears her ancestry like a badge of honor and is acutely aware of her husband's immigrant heritage. For along with the Mill House and land, she has also inherited from her father its history and lineage. In 1747, a distant relative, Nathaniel Dodderidge, had come to

Virginia with Lord Fairfax, an aristocrat who had owned over five mil-
lion acres of forest in the area. Dodderidge was eventually deeded the
land on Back Creek by Fairfax himself.[23] The forest, mountains, and riv-
ers in the area "had never been explored except by the Indians and were
nameless except for their unpronounceable Indian names" (26). Implicit
in the story of the Dodderidge acquisition of that land is the indifferent
dismissal and ultimate displacement of the local native population. Thus
Sapphira's position, her privileged place, has been purchased at great cost
to the Other, Native Americans as well as blacks.

Her current mode of life has been further determined by the ideological constructs of customs and manners. Aware that her place in society will be compromised by her marriage to Henry Colbert, Sapphira
builds a new home at the Mill Farm, then moves her household possessions and an entourage of slaves, choosing "Back Creek for her place of
exile" (25). But her exile signifies more than a separation from her privileged position in society. It also suggests—as it did for Myra Henshawe—
exile from the self. Just as the South grew tired of defending its position
throughout the civilized world, withdrawing from its critics and the outside forces and retreating into what C. Vann Woodward calls "an isola-
tionism of spirit,"[24] Sapphira, too, unable to bear social stigma, chooses
to escape.

Unlike Sapphira, Henry Colbert does question the institution of
slavery. But rather than seek critical inquiry into the consequences of
corrosive power structures, he turns to religious doctrines that neither
condemn nor condone slavery. Although we are told he reads with his
mind as well as his eyes, his is a mind prone to rationalization and justification. He is, after all, a part of the system, literally wed to it. He has
chosen to live within its boundaries, both physically, economically, and,
although he may not wish to acknowledge it, politically as well. The trou-
bling contradictions he claims to encounter in the Bible and in his readings of Bunyan are extensions of his own unwillingness to take sides in
the issue.

Henry Colbert has, to some degree, the aesthetic and moral sensibility absent in his wife, but it is dangerously compromised by his need to
incorporate chattel slavery into his aesthetic sensibility rather than to
condemn it. He knows he has a legal right to free Sapphira's slaves but

does not wish to insult his wife. Moreover, he rationalizes that such an act would be "an injustice to the slaves themselves" because they have "never learned to take care of themselves or to provide for tomorrow" (108).

Henry's justifications run perilously close to the arguments presented in both antebellum and early postbellum plantation narratives and in popular essays of that era. William Gilmore Simms, in an essay in the *Southern Literary Messenger,* defined liberty by the moral and intellectual capability of the mind: "*He is a freeman, whatever his condition, who fills his proper place. He is a slave only, who is forced into a position in society below the claims of his intellect. He cannot but be a tyrant who is found in a position for which his mind is unprepared, and to which it is inferior.*"[25] Simms further believed it was the slaveholders' God-given duty to assume "the moral and animal guardianship of an ignorant and irresponsible people under their control. . . . *Providence,*" he argued, "*has placed [the African slave] in our hands, for his good, and has paid us from his labor for our guardianship.*"[26]

Henry Colbert echoes Simms when he tells Sapphira, "Sometimes keeping people in their place is being good to them" (268). As if to substantiate this argument, we learn in the epilogue that after Sapphira's death Henry frees all the slaves, yet not one of them wants to leave—a classic postbellum pastoral plantation motif. Even after he finds some of them good positions elsewhere, Till tells us, "they kep' makin' excuse to stay on" (288). Moreover, Tap, the boy who once worked in the mill, later gets into a brawl, kills a man and is hanged because according to the local people, "he hadn't been able to stand his freedom" (290). Implicit in this statement is an endorsement of Simms's ideological vision of the responsible and benevolent master who is there to protect those in his charge—a decidedly pastoral, as well as Carlylian concept, which seems to suggest that Cather's own position, although she did not condone slavery, was sympathetic to the concept of the privileged class caring for the less fortunate. We should consider, however, that Cather was probably familiar with the works of Simms—certainly with the works of his protégé John Esten Cooke—and also with the process of rationalization people of the antebellum South employed in order to justify chattel slavery. Thus it seems probable that the character of Henry Colbert is in-

tended to exemplify Cather's understanding of the mind's need for justification and capacity for self-deception rather than her own political
sympathies.

Further supporting this antebellum ideology is Henry's recalling the
time three years earlier when he offered his head mill-hand Sampson his
freedom. Sampson had pleaded a sound case for why he should stay on
at the mill, claiming among other things that he could not keep his
family as well in the city as he could at the Mill Farm. Henry is easily,
and not surprisingly, won over by Sampson's argument because it is exactly what he wants to hear, confirmation that he has been looking out
for his mill-hand's best interest. Later, he turns again to the Bible where
he reads how Joseph, Daniel, and the prophets had once been slaves. No-
where in the Bible is slavery actually condemned, he reasons, then further extends his justification to the broad generalization that in many
ways no one was free. "If Lizzie, the cook, was in bonds to Sapphira, was
she not almost equally in bonds to Lizzie?" (110).

Ironically, Henry's justification bears a certain truth, but not in the
way he intends. Sapphira is in fact bound to Lizzie, likewise to Till, Jezebel, and the others, but in a destructively parasitic way. Her privileged
situation has deteriorated to the point at which her control, her power,
can only be exerted through devious and manipulative means. Crippled, Sapphira must be carried by servants almost everywhere she
goes—"carried in her chair" (101) on the way to Jezebel's funeral and later
"carried out of the graveyard" (103). Yet, metaphorically, they have been
carrying her all along. Sapphira's loss of power is further manifested in
her growing paranoia. Thus she chooses to project her anger at Nancy
rather than at the impending failure of the very system by which she has
always been supported.

This imminent doom is evident in Cather's decision to set the novel
in 1856. For in May of that year John Brown made his first lethal attack
on those who supported slavery. The Pottawatomie massacre in Kansas,
in which Brown and seven other men slaughtered innocent people, "left
a deep trauma in the minds of the people."[27] Tensions mounted, and
there was constant fear of "servile insurrection." Slave owners knew well
enough that uprisings of this nature would of necessity be "secret, sud-
den, and extremely bloody, sparing neither men, women, nor children."[28]
Although the Pottawatomie massacre took place in May, two months af-

ter Cather's story begins, John Brown had already begun to undermine the slave system through his "guerrilla warfare"[29] and fiery outbursts as early as 1855. The stage, so to speak, had already been set. Not surprisingly, then, Sapphira's fears seem to reach a crisis point during the month of April, as if in anticipation of a coming insurrection.

Sapphira's paranoia begins to evolve into irrational fear and anger. Even her name, as Cather, a classics scholar, would have known, suggests her emotional state: the Latin word for *ire* is *ira.*[30] But Sapphira has learned how to contain her emotions because it is expected of someone in her position. Thus feeling threatened by something unnamable, unable to express her frustration and outrage over her physical incapacity, alienated from any inner source of spiritual comfort, Sapphira must seek a scapegoat for the disorder that threatens her otherwise controlled and orderly world. As Cather wrote in a letter to Viola Roseboro, she had been attempting in this novel to capture something pervasive and evil in the quotidian domesticity of antebellum Virginia, something she called "the Terrible."[31] My own contention is that Cather's "Terrible" equates to Jefferson's fear of slave ownership as a source of corruption of the mind, a disintegration of moral values. In his review of *Sapphira and the Slave Girl,* Henry Seidel Canby insightfully observes that "Cather is not writing a melodrama of slavery and seduction, but recreating, with subtle selection of incident, a society and a culture and a sociology in which a conflict of morals and of philosophies produces an inner, ever more tightly-coiled spring."[32] Canby's "inner, ever more tightly-coiled spring" refers here to the tensions within the society/culture, as evidenced in the ideological clash between Sapphira and her daughter Rachel, as well as in Henry's precautionary but ineffectual fence-sitting. But Canby's metaphor is perhaps even more applicable to the mental state of the individual slave owner, in this case Sapphira herself. Her position has always been—in keeping with the antebellum ideology of her time—that slavery was justifiable as long as the slaveholders believed they were fulfilling, in Simms's words, "a sacred duty, undertaken to God and man alike,"[33] to be the guardians of the men and women in their charge. Such a position in the antebellum Southern mind is well within the tradition of noblesse oblige. But Sapphira's situation has been drastically altered by her illness. She is now dependent on those whom she had always understood were under her care. Such knowledge, had she allowed herself to comprehend its significance fully, would have undermined a lifetime of social conditioning. The reality, of course, as Faulkner, Warren, Tate, and others understood, is that the system had always been parasitic, relying on slave labor for its economic existence.[34] That Cather, too, understood the irony of the situation is evident in the previously mentioned "carried" metaphors. Sapphira, however, denies, or rejects, such knowledge. Instead, she reconfigures her power constructs to reinforce her privileged position and to maintain order. The result is corrosive. She becomes the reification of Thomas Jefferson's apocalyptic vision. "The Terrible" has been unleashed, and Sapphira's power takes the form of Machiavellian machinations, which at first glance appear to be motivated by jealousy and indignity,[35] the latter initiated by Henry's casual conversation with Nancy, wherein he breaches Southern etiquette by speaking to her as an equal. What Sapphira witnesses in this exchange is a potential fissure in a system that is already under attack by abolitionist forces. The threat is all the greater since Sapphira, who fully comprehends her husband's moral confusion, perceives Henry to be leaning toward a more democratic relationship with her slaves.

Terrors begin to haunt Sapphira as she lies alone at night, reliving her father's illness and her inability to show him warmth or compassion toward the end of his life. Long suppressed emotions begin to surface, leaving her feeling "lonely and wretched and injured" (105). When she attempts to draw on her usual strength it fails her, sending her into a tailspin of paranoia that takes the form of an imagined household insurrection. She believes her servants are deceiving her, and "the thought of being befooled, hoodwinked in any way" is "unendurable to her" (106). Even the loyal Till is under suspicion. Only when Sapphira finally rings the chamber bell, bringing Till instantly to her bedside, offering comfort and relief from physical pain by bathing Sapphira's swollen ankles in hot water and massaging her knees, is order restored. Sapphira's "shattered, treacherous house" is once again safe (106–7). But like Roderick Usher's ancestral mansion, we suspect Sapphira's shattered, treacherous house now, too, bears a fissure.[36] Metaphorically, Sapphira's house, like Godfrey St. Peter's and Roderick Usher's (and like the crack in Bartley Alexander's bridge), also signifies the human mind.

Alert to her own vulnerabilities, Sapphira must fight all the harder not to succumb to weakness. To show distress would undermine her ability to rule her household and control the slave population under her charge. With Martin's arrival, she seems to regain her composure and self-assurance. For she now has an ally, although he too is unaware of his place in her grand scheme, her plan to bring about Nancy's fall. But just as Jim Burden contributes to the destruction of his edenic Midwest through his position as legal counsel to a great Western railroad, Sapphira sets events in motion that can only serve to hasten the impending loss of her antebellum culture. In this manner, she is both creator of her Eden and the serpent in its garden: savior and serpent, the "Double S." By introducing the sexual component (Martin), through which she intends to bring about Nancy's fall from grace, she assumes the role of the snake. As evident from Cather's previous novels, particularly *O Pioneers!*, sex almost always forebodes chaos in an otherwise orderly world. It is a destructive force in the garden.

But Sapphira's devious plan to have Martin rob Nancy of her innocence is ambiguous at best. Jealousy seems an unlikely motive. For long before she overhears Lizzie suggesting that the relationship between Henry and Nancy is sexual (an accusation Nancy firmly denies), Sapphira has (a full thirty pages earlier) already written to Henry's nephew Martin asking him to spend some time at the Mill Farm. We wonder, then, just what Sapphira has to gain by bringing Martin to the farm to seduce Nancy. The answer, I believe, is evident in the first paragraph of the book. The story opens, "Henry Colbert, the miller, always breakfasted with his wife—beyond that he appeared irregularly at the family table" (3). From the first sentence the roles of the two main characters are established. Sapphira, although the mistress of Mill Farm, is still Henry's "wife," suggesting a secondary and subordinate position. Furthermore, Henry may pay lip service to her position—"You're the master here, and I'm the miller. And that's how I like it to be" (50)—but he has his own methods of control. Henry's is a passive/aggressive personality. His power lies in his maddening ability to do quietly exactly as he pleases. Thus his appearances at the family table are irregular, and Sapphira, we learn (also in the first paragraph) never questions his whereabouts. We discern, however, from conversations, that Sapphira would welcome his company more often. Furthermore, Henry may believe it would be a disservice to his wife to free her slaves, but he has nevertheless offered Sampson his freedom. He will not allow Sapphira to sell Nancy, arguing that the Colberts do not sell their slaves, but we later learn that Sapphira sold a number of slaves after moving to the Mill House to help Henry get set up in business. The slaves, we are led to understand, returned to Loudon County, which had been their original home. What is left unsaid, of course, is that although they have gone back to their old territory, they have nonetheless been sold and are therefore the chattel of new masters. There is nothing humane in this act. Yet we are led to believe the circumstances of this situation are somehow different. On closer examination, however, Henry's motives reveal his self-interest. The difference between selling Nancy and the previous slaves is that with the former situation Henry stands to lose a good housekeeper, a well-trained servant who knows exactly how he wishes things to be done, whereas the latter financially benefited his business.

For all his alleged affection for Nancy, which he wishes to believe is merely paternal, Henry deserts her when her dilemma threatens his sense of moral order and his aesthetic ideal. For just as Jim Burden imposes his mythopoeic vision on Ántonia, just as Niel Herbert creates his imaginative idealization of Marian Forrester, Henry Colbert appropriates Bunyan's "Mercy, Christiana's sweet companion" (67) to accommodate his own mythic vision of Nancy Till. Similarly, just as Jim Burden's image of Ántonia is threatened by an awareness of her sexuality, and Niel Herbert's ideal of Marian crumbles when he realizes she is having an affair, Henry Colbert refuses to see Nancy when he learns she is in danger of being sexually compromised by his nephew Martin. The incident forces him to confront his true feelings for Nancy. Yet even though the "Colbert in him threaten[s] to raise its head after long hibernation" (209), Henry knows he would never betray the girl's trust by seducing her. But realizing their relationship can never be the same, he chooses instead to avoid her.

Believing that it would be wrong to interfere with his wife's "property," Henry Colbert declines to assist Rachel in plotting Nancy's escape. But he nevertheless devises a plan that requires his own daughter to become a thief. On the night Rachel slips up to the open window and takes the money he has left in his coat pocket, Henry imagines Nancy going "up out of Egypt to a better land" where she will learn to take care of herself. He knows that Sapphira's slaves are "better cared for, better fed and better clothed, than the poor whites in the mountains," but he is fully aware that not one of the mountain folk would trade places with his head miller Sampson (229).

Although not as self-centered as his wife, Henry does look out for his own best interest. In his passive/aggressive way, he is a viable opponent for the imperious, inflexible Sapphira. Thus Sapphira, obviously aware of her husband's ambiguous position regarding the slaves, his ability to free them at will, his respect for his mill-hand Sampson, and his growing affection for Nancy, must find a means to shift the balance of power in her own favor or stand by while her antebellum world splits apart.

Despite Henry's family history, the roguish behavior of his brothers, the "bad blood" of the Colbert men (191), Sapphira knows all too well that he is an honorable man, acknowledging she "had married the only Colbert who had a conscience," even sometimes wishing "he hadn't quite so much" (108). Rather than an attempt to foil a potentially sexual relationship between Henry and Nancy, her real purpose is to make clear to whom Nancy belongs. This issue is a matter of ownership and control. Nancy is a pawn in a cultural tug-of-war. Just as Sapphira married off Till to a "capon man" so that Till would not have children to distract her from her duties to her mistress, she will likewise attempt to orchestrate Nancy's fall from innocence.

Concomitant with her concern over Henry's potentially democratic defection is Sapphira's contained outrage over her daughter's abolitionist sympathies. Rachel Blake is, on the surface, Sapphira's opposite. She eschews wealth and position, has joined the Baptist church, chooses to enter her mother's home by the back door, and above all rejects the institution of chattel slavery. But Rachel is nonetheless a product of the early years she spent in her mother's home (as was Cather), and the effects of the chattel system have shaped and molded her attitudes and beliefs just as they have Sapphira's, Henry's, and Martin's. Rachel habitually speaks to her mother's slaves "with a resolute cheerfulness which she [does] not always feel" (17). She calls Nancy "child," intending to suggest innocence, while simultaneously upholding the belief that slaves are childlike and therefore need to be looked after. Indeed, even the narrative description of Nancy seems to support this view. In the same scene, Nancy uses a child's iron, and her "slender hands" are compared to those of a child (18).

Unlike Mrs. Bywaters, an outspoken abolitionist, Rachel is not politically involved. She lives and moves within the system, most likely sharing in the fruits of slave labor, yet does nothing to change it until she is approached by Nancy, who needs her help. Furthermore, Rachel appears to have little trouble with the way her mother treats the slaves because Sapphira has, for the most part, dealt with them kindly and fairly. Although realizing her mother's inconsistencies, Rachel still admires her kindness: "her indulgence with Tansy Dave, her real affection for Till and old Jezebel, her patience with Sampson's lazy wife" (220), her affectionate joking with her black servants at the Christmas party, and her doctoring of the sick. Rachel concedes that Sapphira believes in the system, as do her slaves, especially Till. Yet, she concludes, "it ain't right" (221). Rachel's disclaimer that she does not know how to deal with slaves because she has never owned one is discredited by the fact that she has been raised in a home where slaves are indeed owned. That she herself does not in the present own slaves hardly precludes her knowledge of "how to deal with them" (15). For Rachel, "It was the *owning* that was wrong" (137). And although she has always hated her mother's sharp reprimands to the servants, the question arises whether Sapphira would have treated the servants any differently if they had been hired help. (One calls to mind Thea Kronborg's imperious and scolding attitude toward her indifferent housekeeper.) Customs and manners in Sapphira's culture determine how the privileged classes relate to others, whether they are slaves or free mountain women. Thus Sapphira will nurse and care for her slaves but does not associate with the mountain folk. Rachel, however, applies these same skills to those living in the mountains. She tends the sick and brings food and clothing to the poor. Yet despite her down-home mode of dress and her ascetic lifestyle, she nevertheless carries on the tradition of noblesse oblige, a mark of her breeding and her class. Having saved one of the mountain boys, Casper Flight, from his bullying Keyser cousins, she decides to have a talk with the Reverend Fairfield, whose school Casper attends, believing the boy might be better off not attending school (the source of his cousins' behavior toward him). Just as Henry worries that freeing the slaves would jeopardize their welfare, Rachel wonders if it is wise to encourage Casper, believing he is not "strong enough to master what's around him" (130). For Rachel, it is only the "owning" that is abhorrent.

Indeed, no one in this system has been left untouched by the institution of chattel slavery. Even the servants appear to be satisfied with the status quo. As Rachel notes, "They believe in it" (221). Till considers herself a Dodderidge. Her loyalty has always been to the mistress of the house. She has been "trained," as have Nancy and the other servants, for her position. As housekeeper, Till has her own hierarchical paradigm. Her attitude toward Lizzie, Bluebell, and the slaves who work the mill and farm, is often condescending, snobbish, and downright patronizing. She considers the mountain folk poor white trash. She has been so indoctrinated that she wishes only to be "respectable and wellplaced" (72). For the most part, she appears to accept her present situation. Yet her inner thoughts often belie the surface appearance: "Sitting on the doorstep huddled in her quilt, Till heard a mournful sound come from the deep woods across the creek: the first whippoorwill. She sighed. How she hated the call of that bird! Every spring she had to listen to it, coming out of this resigned, unstirring back-country. Another spring, and here she still was, by the millpond and the damp meadows" (73). Like her mistress, Till lives in exile, hidden away in the deep-wooded mountains. She believes she was intended for better things. Trained by an English housekeeper, Till despairs over wasting her skills in this backwoods wilderness. Yet she never questions the system that impedes her dreams. If she were free, she could seek a position in a fine house "where people of some account lived" (73) and where she could use her best skills. The mournful cry of the whippoorwill stirs her own pain and resignation, and just as Sapphira transforms Nancy into a scapegoat for her own fear and anger, Till transforms the call of the whippoorwill into an object of hatred rather than confront the full reality of her own condition. In this respect, she resembles her mistress. Like Sapphira, she has learned to bury conflicting emotions; she eschews critical thought in favor of the familiar. Not wishing to stir these familiar waters, she elects not to come to her daughter's aid when the girl is being pursued by Martin, choosing instead to allow the drama to play out its own course.

Similarly, all of the slaves at Mill Farm pretend not to see Nancy's imminent danger, or to assist her. To do so would prove disloyal to their mistress, a decidedly feudal, and by extension pastoral, attitude.[37] Like Till and the others, Henry also maintains a laissez-faire position regarding both Nancy and the slave system itself. He would leave the issue of slavery to God who "moves in a mysterious way" (111), and he trusts that "the Lord had already chosen His heralds and His captains, and a morning would break when all the black slaves would be free" (112). Such a morning does indeed break, and the Lord's herald is Rachel Blake. The insurrection Sapphira has dreaded is within her own ranks. Although this rebellion is on a small scale, it nevertheless foreshadows the historical events to follow.

But even Nancy, who with Rachel Blake's help now has an opportunity to escape, has been, like Till, so indoctrinated into the system that freedom seems inconceivable to her. She resists leaving the Mill Farm, the only home she has known, and her mode of transport signifies what this exile truly means to her. Hidden in a wagon used for carrying coffins, transported to a ferry where a ferryman waits to carry her to the other side (like Charon ferrying her across the river Styx), Nancy's dispossession is linked symbolically with death, as it was for Godfrey St. Peter and for nine-year-old Willa Cather. Despite the dangers that await her back at the Mill Farm, Nancy begs Rachel Blake to take her home where she can be among her own people. "I can't bear it to belong nowheres" (237), she tells Rachel. Already her mind is "frozen with homesickness and dread" (237). Knowing how difficult Cather's own exile had been, how it had thematically woven its way throughout her fiction, we can understand that while escape with its resultant new life is Nancy's only recourse, she also perceives it as an unjustified treatment for something over which she has no control. Control is the operative word here. For just as Cather and her mother had no say in their exile from Virginia in 1883, Nancy, likewise caught up in a system that sees her as powerless, must acquiesce in the end. Indeed, the epilogue, which takes place twenty-five years later, reinforces the view that the escape was the much needed impetus to Nancy's growth. Exile has allowed her to claim herself and her potential (as it eventually did for Cather). When Nancy returns from Canada for a visit to Back Creek, she has become a fine, strong, and independent woman.

Rachel's course of action, her decision to assist Nancy, then, is on the one hand an act of defiance against the system but on the other an act of defiance against her own mother, an act for which she pays dearly. For Sapphira, seeing in her daughter's dissent the beginning of the end of her world, asks Rachel not to come to the Mill Farm again. Later, drawn

together through crisis and loss, Rachel and Sapphira are eventually re-
united, as are Till and Nancy in the epilogue. For this story is also one
of forgiveness, a feminine version of the prodigal son. The Sapphira we
see at the end of the book has reconciled herself to the inevitability of
her impending death, an end that adumbrates the close of the antebellum era, the demise of the Old South. Without apology, without ever
lowering "her flag" (268), Sapphira simply acknowledges to Henry, "We
would all do better if we had our lives to live over again" (269). But she
makes it clear that they have enjoyed many happy years at Mill Farm and
would never have been as content anywhere else. Her death, as we later
learn in the epilogue, is quiet and dignified. Alone in her chair, surrounded by candles, Sapphira looks out onto the snow-covered lilac arbor. She does not ring the bell for Till, preferring in the end to be alone.
Hers is the death Myra Henshawe, exiled from her ancestral past and
social position, had longed for and been denied.

The final words in the book are spoken by Till, and at first we are
reminded of Faulkner's *The Sound and the Fury*, where the black characters dominate the last page, ending with DILSEY followed by a simple,
dignified "They endured."[38] But Till's final words only serve to confirm
her devotion to her mistress, and by implication, her devotion to the
chattel system: "Mrs. Matchem, down at the old place, never got over it
that Miss Sapphy didn't buy in Chestnut Hill an' live like a lady, 'stead a'
leavin' it to run down under the Bushwell's, an herself comin' out here
where nobody was anybody much" (295). Furthermore, although Cather
gives the last words of the story to Till, the last words of the text are
Cather's. In a subtle way she seemed to be reasserting her authorial position, reclaiming the story, when she added the brief disclaimer regarding the names of her characters, many of which were common surnames
in Frederick County, Virginia, and contending that the characters were
not based on any of these people. The words "The End" follow Till's
speech. But the last words to appear on the text page are the author's own
name.

*Sapphira and the Slave Girl* is, after all, a story based in part on
Cather's ancestral past. And although she expressed concern that she had
"made an artistic error in bringing herself into the story" as the five-
year-old child eagerly awaiting Nancy's visit,[39] it seems fitting that she
should appear in the epilogue after being absent from the South for so

many years. In the epilogue, she could now step forward in full view of the literary establishment to reclaim her past. As the child in this last segment of the story, Cather lets us experience the past alive in the present as it must have seemed to her then. Her presence in the story reminds us, as Minrose Gwin notes, that "we can never really know the past, yet at the same time we cannot escape it."[40] Long before Cather was born, Southern writer William Gilmore Simms believed, as C. Hugh Holman observed, "the greatest source of historical truth is not in documents but in memory, in the oral traditions of a people."[41] Simms may have perpetuated the [past]oral plantation myth during the antebellum era, but his view of history and memory seems to have endured, finding its way into the writings of Faulkner, Warren, Tate, Welty, and many other twentieth-century Southern writers, or those, like Cather, whose Southern sensibility somehow brought them to the same place.

Cather's own ambiguous position on the slave issue hardly comes as a surprise. Her racial attitudes have created a continual paradox throughout this study. What seems clear from the novel is that, like Rachel Blake, Cather too condemned the owning. But as numerous recent critics have noted, the treatment of blacks in *Sapphira and the Slave Girl*, as viewed from our own time frame, nevertheless remains problematic. Cather often falls into an uncomfortable stereotyping of blacks and of slavery (especially concerning the former slaves' attitudes toward their freedom), even though her intention seems to have been to subvert stereotypical behavior. One might argue that white writers of that era were poorly informed about minority groups, those who had been silenced for so long and who had kept their opinions buried within themselves, tolerating the stereotypes perpetuated by the privileged classes. But, in fact, during the time Cather lived on Bank Street, the Harlem Renaissance was at its height, producing the strong literary voices of W. E. B. DuBois, Langston Hughes, Claude McKay, and later, Zora Neale Hurston. In 1940, the year *Sapphira* was published, Richard Wright's *Native Son* would finally explode many of those stereotypes. But whether Cather was familiar with or even read the works of these authors remains a mystery.

She had been raised on a different literature, the antebellum and postbellum voice of one of her family's favorite authors, John Esten Cooke, among others. She had known the postbellum Uncle Remus stories of Joel Chandler Harris, and perhaps most influential of all, stories of her own ancestral past. Moreover, in 1940, the South was still segregated. Raised in a Southern family, Cather simply did not socialize with blacks. The only known occasion when she sat down with a black person was when she met Paul Robeson one evening at the Menuhins' home.[42] Slavery for Cather was "neither a torture prison nor a benevolent training school. It had had its pleasant domestic surfaces," as she wrote to Ferris Greenslet in response to his letter praising *Sapphira,* adding that she never thought of Till "as a person to be pitied."[43] As James Woodress points out, Cather was not attempting "to write a polemic against slavery," an act that would have "been out of character and inappropriate in 1940."[44] Still we must acknowledge, as does Toni Morrison, that while Cather "may not have arrived safely, like Nancy, . . . to her credit she did undertake the dangerous journey."[45]

We know, too, that hierarchical power structures and their abuse continued to pique her imaginative curiosity. For although *Sapphira and the Slave Girl* was to become her last published novel, Cather had begun work on another book before her death in 1947, tentatively titled *Hard Punishments.* The story takes place in Avignon during the reign of Benedict XII.[46] The central characters are two boys from different classes who have both been victims of medieval injustice. Unfortunately, at Cather's request, Edith Lewis destroyed the manuscript following Cather's death, although four pages were later recovered.[47] From what little we know about *Hard Punishments,* it appears that Cather planned once again to explore the abuse of power within a feudal society.

In her last published novel, Cather's literary journey brought her back to the Southern ancestral roots from which she had been estranged for so many years. The direction may not have always been apparent, but one thread had continued to guide her through the labyrinth, like Ariadne's ball of twine. That thread was Willa Cather's pastoral vision. Although she had not lived in the South for many years, her use of pastoral modes and the course of her journey paralleled a direction unique to Southern literature: from the pastoral ideal, to alienation and disillusionment, and finally to historical reconciliation—an acceptance of her own historical past and a reclamation of her ancestral roots.

Remembering the "good six pounds" of manuscript Cather discarded when writing *Sapphira and the Slave Girl,* "the flooding force of a great wealth of impressions,"[48] later tossed aside, we cannot help but feel the loss of all those additional stories that had been stored for so many years in her memory, stories which I believe would have revealed further information on Cather's Southern background and its effects on her work. In the end, though, Cather chose to render fully the Old South with all its flaws; she never condemned the behavior of her characters, leaving both the South and Sapphira unconquered and proud. Like her imperious and complex heroine, we might say of Cather, as well, "she never lowered her flag."

# Notes

## Preface

1. The postbellum era referred to in this study covers only that period directly after the Civil War to the early Southern Renaissance period between 1920 and 1940.

2. According to Elizabeth Shepley Sergeant, Cather also had little tolerance for sociological fiction. See Elizabeth Shepley Sergeant, *Willa Cather: A Memoir* (Philadelphia: Lippincott, 1953; reprint, Athens: Ohio University Press, 1992), 176.

## Introduction

1. James Woodress, *Willa Cather: A Literary Life* (Lincoln: University of Nebraska Press, 1987; Bison Book, 1989), 28.

2. Willa Cather to Elizabeth Shepley Sergeant, 12 September 1913. Paraphrased in Hermione Lee, *Willa Cather: Double Lives* (New York: Pantheon Books, 1989), 357.

3. Edith Lewis, *Willa Cather Living: A Personal Record* (New York: Alfred A. Knopf, 1953), 182.

4. E. K. Brown finds Cather's "dismissal of the experiences of early childhood" remarkable. He bases Cather's rejection of these early formative years, as have other critics, on the quotation that appeared in the *Omaha Bee* interview. E. K. Brown, *Willa Cather: A Critical Biography*, completed by Leon Edel (New York: Alfred A. Knopf, 1953; reprint, Lincoln: University of Nebraska Press, Bison Book, 1987), 3.

5. For an in-depth discussion of Cather's landscapes, see Laura Winters, *Willa Cather: Landscape and Exile* (Selinsgrove, PA: Susquehanna University Press, 1993).

6. Eudora Welty, "The House of Willa Cather," *The Eye of the Story: Selected Essays and Reviews* (New York: Random House, 1977), 47, 43.

7. Lewis, 23.

8. Welty, 45.

9. Bernice Slote, "First Principles: The Kingdom of Art," *The Kingdom of Art: Willa Cather's First Principles and Critical Statements, 1893–1896*, ed. Bernice Slote (Lincoln: University of Nebraska Press, 1966), 104–5.

10. These various stages appear in Lewis P. Simpson, *The Dispossessed Garden*, and are discussed in depth throughout his text. See Lewis P. Simpson, *The Dispossessed Garden: Pastoral and History in Southern Literature* (Athens: University of Georgia Press, 1975).

11. Lucinda Hardwick MacKethan, *The Dream of Arcady: Place and Time in Southern Literature* (Baton Rouge: Louisiana State University Press, 1980), 4.

12. E. K. Brown perceives the events surrounding Cather's Virginia childhood as only "a prelude to her years of experience and preparation," rather than "a part of them." Brown, 5.

13. Middleton uses the scientific term "vacuole" as a way of defining the intentional gaps Cather leaves in the text for her readers. See Jo Ann Middleton, *Willa Cather's Modernism: A Study of Style and Technique* (Rutherford, NJ: Fairleigh Dickinson University Press, 1990), 11.

14. Cather defines "the thing not named" as "[w]hatever is felt upon the page without being specifically named there," an "inexplicable presence . . . the overtone divined by the ear but not heard by it, the verbal mood, the emotional aura of the fact or the thing or the deed." See "The Novel Démeublé" in *Not Under Forty* (New York: Alfred A. Knopf, 1922; Lincoln: University of Nebraska Press, Bison Book, 1988), 50; and *Willa Cather on Writing: Critical Studies on Writing as an Art* (New York: Alfred A. Knopf, 1920; Lincoln: University of Nebraska Press, Bison Book, 1988), 41–42.

15. Simpson, 2.

16. Elizabeth Jane Harrison, *Female Pastoral: Women Writers Re-Visioning the American South* (Knoxville: University of Tennessee Press, 1991), 2.

17. MacKethan, 16.

18. Simpson, 2. Simpson's discussion on the pastoral focuses on the New World as the redemptive garden, rather than on Virgilian pastoral. Nevertheless, this study will incorporate both versions.

19. Ibid., 13.

20. Ibid., 20.

21. Ibid., 38–39.

22. Elizabeth Harrison has noted that Richard King, Lewis Simpson, and other respected scholars focus on this form of pastoral as prominent for the period without acknowledging the fiction written by women and African Americans that works against it. See Harrison, 5.

23. Raymond Williams, *The Country and the City* (New York: Oxford University Press, 1973), 32.

24. MacKethan, 9.

25. Whereas antebellum plantation pastorals presented an idyllic, cultured, and graceful world where master and slave lived in complete harmony, the postbel-

lum plantation myths cultivated a nostalgia for the loss of this former way of life that was ostensibly shared by both master and former slave.

26. Merrill Maguire Skaggs, *The Folk of Southern Fiction* (Athens: University of Georgia Press, 1972), 4.

27. Ibid.

28. Williams, 17.

29. C. Vann Woodward, *The Burden of Southern History* (Baton Rouge: Louisiana State University Press, 1960), 19.

30. Francis Pendleton Gaines, *The Southern Plantation: A Study in the Development and the Accuracy of a Tradition* (New York: Columbia University Press, 1924; Gloucester, MA: Peter Smith, 1962), 63.

31. Ibid., 210.

32. Although Cather does not return to the South as her setting until her last novel, Southern characters do appear in some of her books. Moreover, the semi-autobiographical short story "Old Mrs. Harris" is about a Southern family that has relocated in the Midwest.

## 1. Cather's Southern Heritage and Pastoral Origins

1. Sources for biographical history are Bennett, E. K. Brown, Lee, Lewis, O'Brien, Sergeant, and Woodress.

2. David Stouck, *Willa Cather's Imagination* (Lincoln: University of Nebraska Press, 1975), 37.

3. C. Hugh Holman, *The Roots of Southern Writing: Essays on the Literature of the American South* (Athens: University of Georgia Press, 1972), 1.

4. Merrill Maguire Skaggs, *After the World Broke in Two: The Later Novels of Willa Cather* (Charlottesville: University Press of Virginia, 1990), 16.

5. Lee, 16.

6. Ibid.

7. According to Susan and David Parry, current owners of Willow Shade, the Cather homestead consisted of 331 acres.

8. Although Edith Lewis refers to the house as a "three-story brick mansion," the structure, though large and impressive, was actually two stories with an English basement. See Lewis, 4.

9. Woodress, 13.

10. Sergeant, *Memoir*, 46–47.

11. According to James Woodress, all three of Rachel Boak's sons fought for the Confederacy. See Woodress, 18. However, E. K. Brown contends that one of the sons died before age twenty, and only the two remaining sons fought in the Civil War. See Brown, 15.

12. Woodress, 16.

13. Many of these customs would later appear in "Old Mrs. Harris" and *Sapphira and the Slave Girl*, for example, Victoria Templeton's pampered treatment, Mr. Templeton's gentlemanly ways and his lack of business skill (see also Cather's sketch of the Southern gentleman based on her father [*WP* 20-21]), Mrs. Harris's position as housekeeper, and the tradition of noblesse oblige.

14. Lewis, 9-10. It is especially interesting that the young Willa, while assuming the roll of Cato, simultaneously imagined the slave reminding Cato that he is only a man, as if the two sides of her own dichotomous nature were discoursing on the subject of class.

15. Mildred R. Bennett, *The World of Willa Cather* (New York: Dodd, Mead and Company, 1951), 6. According to Mildred Bennett, Henry Seibert may have been the prototype for the fictional Henry Colbert in *Sapphira and the Slave Girl*. Other accounts suggest that Cather's great-grandmother Seibert was the prototype for Sapphira Colbert.

16. I am grateful to Susan and David Parry, current owners of Willow Shade, for sharing their census data and knowledge of Tina Skinner's article, "Freed Slaves Found Mecca in Local Area," *Winchester Star*, 1 February 1992. See Susan Parry, "The Cather Home Place: Willow Shade in Memory and Reality," Paper read at the Fifth International Willa Cather Seminar, 19-26 June 1993, at Hastings College, Hastings, Nebraska.

17. Cather's poem "Poor Marty," a tribute to Marjorie Anderson, acknowledges that like many poor whites who worked for well-to-do families, she worked for her room and board: "Hire nor wages did she draw" (*ATOP*, 70).

18. Lewis, 12.

19. E. K. Brown, 12, 16.

20. Fisher quoted in E. K. Brown, 4.

21. According to historical sociologist Robert A. Nisbet, these old values included "hierarchy, community, tradition, authority, and the sacred sense of life." See Robert A. Nisbet, *Tradition and Revolt: Historical and Sociological Essays* (New York: Random House, 1968), 4.

22. According to E. K. Brown, those "first nine years of [Cather's] life gave her neither a subject nor a theme." Moreover, during the years when she wrote criticism and reviews, "she scarcely ever chose a Southern subject or concerned herself with a Southern writer." See Brown, 3, 5.

23. Lewis, 12.

24. Willa Cather to Mrs. Ackroyd (granddaughter of Mary Ann Anderson), 16 May 1941, The Barrett Collection, University of Virginia, Charlottesville.

25. Mildred Bennett, "The Childhood Worlds of Willa Cather," *Great Plains Quarterly* 2:4 (1982): 205.

26. Bennett, *World of Willa Cather*, 1.

27. The image of her father as a shepherd remained with Cather throughout her adult years. After Charles Cather died in 1928, Cather commissioned a German company to create a stained-glass window depicting Christ as the good shepherd, holding a lamb, which she donated in her father's memory to the Grace Episcopal Church in Red Cloud.

28. The term *pastoral* reflects myriad interpretations, as previously noted, whereas the term *bucolic* is generally limited to defining a rural landscape. I use the two terms interchangeably only in this latter context.

29. Lewis, 6, 156.

30. Bennett, *World of Willa Cather*, 30.

31. Ibid., 29.

32. Lewis, 8.

33. For a discussion on the aristocratic dimensions of several of Willa Cather's characters, see Patricia Lee Yongue, "Willa Cather's Aristocrats" (Part I and II), *Southern Humanities Review* 14 (1980): 43–56, 111–25.

34. Bennett, *World of Willa Cather*, 29. Like Virginia Cather, Sapphira Colbert "did not welcome visits from anyone" during "her dressing hour" (*SSG* 13).

35. Bernice Slote, "Introduction" to *Uncle Valentine and Other Stories: Willa Cather's Uncollected Short Fiction, 1915–1929*, ed. Bernice Slote (Lincoln: University of Nebraska Press, 1973; Bison Book, 1986), xiii–xiv.

36. Lewis, 13.

37. According to Lewis, Cather "always said she was more like her mother than any other member of the family." See Lewis, 7.

38. According to Mildred Bennett, William Cather, who still owned Willow Shade, refused to rebuild the sheep barn because he wanted both his sons and their families with him in Nebraska. Virginia Cather "did not want to leave her friends, her home, or the mountain countryside," nor did Willa. Thus, by assuming the name William, Cather was also rebelling against the subordinate role women were assigned within a Victorian society where patriarchal rule prevailed. See Mildred Bennett, "The Childhood Worlds of Willa Cather," 205.

39. Charles Cather auctioned off Willow Shade for six thousand dollars, then auctioned their furniture. The Cathers took only a few treasured possessions with them on their journey West. See Woodress, 31.

40. Robert Penn Warren, "The Use of the Past," *New and Selected Essays* (New York: Random House, 1989), 32.

41. Renato Poggioli sees the pastoral retreat into "a double longing after innocence and happiness" as the opposite of the Christian desire for "conversion and regeneration." See Renato Poggioli, "The Oaten Flute," *Harvard Literary Bulletin* 11 (1957): 147. The Christian image of the Garden of Eden, of edenic landscapes, and of a place of hope and renewal, however, have become accepted variations on the

pastoral form, especially as it equates to the American experience of immigration to the New World. Cather's pastoral modes, while strongly influenced by Virgil, still reflect the Christian pastoral, as evident in her edenic garden imagery. Cather's gardens frequently signify places of innocence, rebirth, and natural abundance, or in the case of Godfrey St. Peter's garden, order.

42. Lewis, 8. The phrase "All their ways" seems particularly revealing in light of Lewis's sketch of the rebellious Willa Cather, followed by her commentary on Cather's need to resist the polite, restrictive conventions of the genteel Southern society. Cather's device of employing reversals, it seems, was as much a part of her daily life, as it was her fictional creations.

43. A frequently told story that is indicative of Cather's early rebellion against convention has young Willa horrifying her mother by threatening an old judge who was visiting with her outburst: "I'se a dang'ous nigger, I is!" when he attempted to stroke her hair. See Lewis, 13. While certainly providing evidence of her rebellious nature, the outburst also suggests her family's ambivalent attitude toward blacks.

44. Woodress, 31; Lewis, 7; and E. K. Brown, 22.

45. Sergeant, *Memoir*, 27.

46. Woodress, 112.

47. Willa Cather to Mrs. Ackroyd, 16 May 1941.

48. E. K. Brown claims the first thing Cather did upon returning to Willow Shade was to head right for the spot where she had left her rabbit traps as a child, finding them still intact. See E. K. Brown, 20–21. Photographs are housed in the archives at the Willa Cather Historical Museum, Red Cloud, Nebraska. The photograph of Willa Cather sitting on the front steps of "Auntie Gore's" house is dated 1905. However, no records show that Cather visited the area between 1896 and 1913 (the time of her second trip). The clothes she wears in the photograph are the same as those she is wearing in the other 1896 photographs taken on her first return trip to Gore.

49. Willa Cather to Mariel Gere, June or July 1896, Archives, Willa Cather Historical Museum, Red Cloud.

50. Sergeant, *Memoir*, 279. In *My Ántonia*, Jim Burden expresses a similar sentiment on returning to Black Hawk years after his departure. "My day in Black Hawk was disappointing," he tells the reader. "Most of my old friends were dead or had moved away" (237).

51. Woodress, 250–51.

52. Sergeant, *Memoir*, 130.

53. During the Red Cloud years, Cather's mother would give birth to two more sons and another daughter.

54. Edith Lewis comments that at the McClung household Cather "enjoyed a tranquility and physical comfort she had probably never before experienced." See

Lewis, 53–54. Yet she describes life at the McClung home much in the same way she describes Cather's early years at Willow Shade. It is hardly surprising that Cather would feel at home in such an environment.

55. Willa Cather to Mrs. Ackroyd, 16 May 1941.

56. Ibid.

57. Woodward, 10.

58. Willa Cather to Mariel Gere, 1 August 1893, Archives, Willa Cather Historical Museum, Red Cloud. Cather places the unusual term "Literary" in quotes, suggesting it was a colloquial expression. Her Aunt Franc, who was a graduate of Smith and Mount Holyoke, headed the local literary group.

59. Woodward, 3.

60. Lewis, 18.

61. Woodress, 28.

62. Lewis, 30.

63. Cather once told Elizabeth Shepley Sergeant one of her fears was that she might die in a cornfield. The sheer expansiveness of the Nebraska plains unnerved her. See Sergeant, *A Memoir*, 59.

64. Lewis, 181–82.

65. Woodress, 28–29.

66. Virginia Verle (Lady Falls) Brown, "Willa Cather and the Southern Genteel Tradition" (Ph.D. diss., Texas Tech University, 1989), xv.

67. Woodress, 69.

68. I am grateful to Polly Duryea for telling me of the existence of this scrapbook, housed in the archives at the Willa Cather Historical Museum in Red Cloud. Cather's selection of cards and pictures pasted in the scrapbook as a child offers a wealth of visual information on her early attitudes.

69. Woodward, 25.

70. Woodress, 210.

71. Sharon O'Brien suggests that Cather deleted "The Namesake" because she no longer identified with male heroes, in this case her uncle William Seibert Boak. She added "Macon Prairie," a tribute to her aunt Jennie Cather Ayer, marking a shift to women role models. See O'Brien, *Willa Cather: The Emerging Voice* (New York: Oxford University Press, 1987; reprint, New York: Ballentine Books, A Fawcett Columbine Book, 1987), 31. It is also possible Cather, after her 1913 visit to Virginia, had become disillusioned with the South, as she indicated in her correspondence with Elizabeth Shepley Sergeant, and no longer thought of herself as Southern or identified with her uncle, a Confederate soldier.

72. Woodward, 15.

73. Cather's loyalties are still a point of confusion for critics. A photograph in Woodress's *Willa Cather: A Literary Life* shows Cather in a "Confederate Army Cap."

The photograph has been reversed with the initials W. C. facing backwards. The same photograph appears in Bennett's *The World of Willa Cather.* Bennett claims it is a Union cap, and that Cather most likely sewed on the initials W. C. herself. Sergeant, on the other hand, simply refers to the hat as a "Civil War cap," which she tells us belonged to Charles Cather, although the initials are W. C. and Cather's father did not fight in the war.

74. Leo Marx, *The Machine in the Garden: Technology and the Pastoral Ideal in America* (New York: Oxford University Press, 1964), 19.

75. *The Georgics and Eclogues of Virgil,* trans. Theodore Chickering Williams (Cambridge: Harvard University Press, 1915), 125.

76. Marx, 20.

77. *Georgics and Eclogues,* 128.

78. Elizabeth Shepley Sergeant, "Willa Cather," *New Republic,* 17 June 1925, 92.

## 2. *Cather's New World Pastorals*

1. Cather's Southern literary predecessors struggled with the difficulty of incorporating chattel slavery into their antebellum and postbellum Arcadia. By transporting her own Arcadia to the West, she was able to avoid this dilemma.

2. After ten years of Nebraska life, Cather still had not resigned herself to what she considered an isolated and culturally bereft existence. Although her University of Nebraska experience brought her into contact with notable and cultured members of Lincoln society, she continued to view life on the Divide and in the town of Red Cloud as the equivalent of being exiled to Siberia.

3. The grim incident in both stories is based on the actual suicide of Francis Sadilek, the father of Anna Sadilek, the prototype for Ántonia Shimerda.

4. Stouck, *Willa Cather's Imagination,* 37.

5. "The essential trick of the old pastoral," according to William Empson, "which was felt to imply a beautiful relation between rich and poor, was to make simple people express strong feelings (felt as the most universal subject, something fundamentally true about everybody) in learned and fashionable language (so that you wrote about the best subject in the best way). From seeing the two sorts of people combined like this you thought better of both; the best parts of both were used." Thus, it was not uncommon for artists to endow their rustic characters with heroic qualities. See William Empson, *Some Versions of Pastoral* (London: Chatto & Windus, 1935), 11–12.

6. Ellen Moers, "Comment," *The Art of Willa Cather,* ed. Bernice Slote and Virginia Faulkner (Lincoln: University of Nebraska Press, 1974), 62.

7. In these later stories, and in many of her later novels, Cather illustrates MacKethan's second pastoral motif, the idealization of "a golden age almost always

associated with childhood," a pastoral of innocence as a psychological retreat. See MacKethan, 4.

8. Lee, 100.

9. Susan Rosowski has noted numerous parallels between *O Pioneers!* and Virgil's *Eclogues*. See Susan J. Rosowski, *The Voyage Perilous: Willa Cather's Romanticism* (Lincoln: University of Nebraska Press, 1986), 47. John Randall also notes the relationships between *O Pioneers!* and the *Eclogues,* but he sees the former more in the tradition of Virgil's *Georgics,* contending that Cather "lacks much of the machinery of the strictly construed eclogue form." See John H. Randall III, "Willa Cather and the Pastoral Tradition," *Five Essays on Willa Cather: The Merrimack Symposium,* ed. John J. Murphy (North Andover, MA: Merrimack College), 81. David Stouck believes *O Pioneers!* to be in the epic tradition rather than the pastoral because the story focuses on the struggles of the immigrants against the hostile forces of nature. See Stouck, *Willa Cather's Imagination,* 23, 25. However, we also need to consider the dynamics of tension, central to Virgilian pastoral, that evolve from these struggles, the contrast, as Raymond Williams notes, between the "pleasures of rural existence" and the "threat of loss and eviction." See Williams, 17.

10. O'Brien, 74.

11. Mildred Bennett relates the story of Cather's trip to France where she "found no difficulty in rhapsodizing over the peasants in the field," yet "was singularly irritated when these self-same noble 'but unwashed' peasants left their field to crowd in beside her in a third-class railway carriage." See Bennett, *World of Willa Cather,* 149.

12. William Empson views the pastoral as a tool of the aristocracy, a means by which it can bridge the hierarchical schism between the upper and working classes by allowing the poor and uneducated to express deep, universal feelings "in learned and fashionable language." See Empson, 11.

13. Elizabeth Harrison contends that the Southern pastoral version of the New Eden served only the Southern white patriarchy, which had designed a culture that associated women and slaves with landownership. See Harrison, 2.

14. John H. Randall III, *The Landscape and the Looking Glass: Willa Cather's Search for Value* (Westport, CT: Greenwood, 1960), 70.

15. In *The Dispossessed Garden* Lewis P. Simpson sees Jefferson's yeoman as no longer subsistent on slave labor and, through his repudiation of the plantation slavery system, purifies the previously corrupted pastoral vision. See Simpson, 31.

16. O'Brien, 432.

17. Lee, 96.

18. MacKethan, 4.

19. O'Brien, 434.

20. Harrison, 9.

21. Harrison sees Southern women writers working in the pastoral tradition as re-visioning the land not as "property," as in the male pastoral plot, "but as an empowering life source." See Harrison, 15.

22. Williams, 22.

23. [Willa Cather], *Willa Cather: A Biographical Sketch/ An English Opinion/ and an Abridged Bibliography* (New York: Knopf, n.d.), 1-2.

24. William Byrd to the Earl of Orrery on his life in Virginia, 1726. See Pierre Marambaud, *William Byrd of Westover, 1674-1744* (Charlottesville: University Press of Virginia, 1971), 146-47.

25. Michael Drayton, *The Works of Michael Drayton*, ed. J. William Hebel, vol. II (New York: Oxford University Press, 1931), 363.

26. See Randall, "Willa Cather and the Pastoral Tradition," 85, for a discussion of Sir Paul Harvey's interpretation of the phrase "Et in Arcadia ego" (" 'Even in Arcadia there am I' [Death]") and its relationship to the deaths of Emil and Marie.

27. Rosowski, 60.

28. Stouck, *Willa Cather's Imagination*, 45.

29. Stouck interprets Cather's affinity with, and interest in, the Native Americans of the Southwest as "a strong undercurrent of thought and feeling which turns away from the romantic dream of selfhood toward the richness and complexity of the perceptual world." He further suggests that in this dimension, Cather is not viewing art "as the product of self-expression but as a process of sympathy for people, places, and events." See David Stouck, "Willa Cather and the Indian Heritage," *Twentieth Century Literature* 22 (1976): 433.

Elizabeth Ammons, on the other hand, points out that no modern-day Native Americans are presented in *The Song of the Lark* or in *The Professor's House*. See Elizabeth Ammons, "Art: Willa Cather, the Woman Writer as Artist, and Humishuma," *Conflicting Stories: American Women Writers at the Turn into the Twentieth Century* (New York: Oxford University Press, 1991), 133. A brief mention of the Navajos living on a nearby reservation and a dismissive statement that they are "not much in the habit of giving or of asking help" (265) does seem to suggest an indifference to the plight of the present-day Native Americans. However, contemporary Native Americans are not the subject of Cather's book.

30. According to Elizabeth Shepley Sergeant, Cather, like her protagonist, also kept some of the potsherds which she later "shamefacedly" showed Sergeant when she returned from her visit to the Southwest. Although Cather felt "it had seemed a sacrilege to take anything for oneself from those cliff dwellings that hung along Walnut Canyon on 'streets' that were hewn from chalky rock," she nevertheless kept her few treasured pieces. See Sergeant, *A Memoir*, 133.

31. Stouck, "Willa Cather and the Indian Heritage," 433.

32. Robert Penn Warren, *All the King's Men* (New York: Harcourt Brace Jovanovich, 1946; A Harvest/HBJ Book, 1982), 438.

33. Ibid., 188.

34. Cather eschewed social activism, a position that drew harsh criticism from the social critics of the 1930s, particularly Granville Hicks and Lionel Trilling. Art—the creation of art—for Cather, always took precedence over everything else, a stance she staunchly defended during her lifetime.

## 3. The Pangs of Disillusionment: Cather's Antipastoral Subtext

1. Simpson, 69.

2. MacKethan, 3.

3. Simpson, 65.

4. Ibid., 70.

5. Rosowski, xiii.

6. Sergeant, *Memoir*, 131.

7. Cather's frequent lament during this time was, "Our present is ruined—but we had a beautiful past," a statement that likewise captures the sentiment of the postbellum era. See Sergeant, *Memoir*, 131.

8. William Faulkner, *Light in August* (Harrison Smith and Robert Haas, 1932; New York: Random House, Vintage Books, 1972), 448.

9. Middleton, 51.

10. Skaggs, *After the World Broke in Two*, 15.

11. Harold E. Toliver, *Pastoral Forms and Attitudes* (Berkeley: University of California Press, 1971), 14.

12. Empson, 12–13.

13. Louis Althusser, "Ideology and Ideological State Apparatuses (Notes towards an investigation)," *Lenin and Philosophy and Other Essays*, trans. Ben Brewster (New York: Monthly Review Press, 1971), 143.

14. Woodward, 13. For further discussion on myths of the Old South, see Gaines, 1–17.

15. Owen Wister's romantic novel *The Virginian*, set in Wyoming in the 1870s and 1880s, tells the story of a handsome, chivalrous, daring Virginian and his heroic adventures and is a classic example of the migration of Southern myths outside the region. See Owen Wister, *The Virginian: A Horseman of the Plains* (New York: Macmillan Company, 1902).

16. I use the term "pioneer aristocrat" interchangeably with John Randall's "natural aristocrat."

17. Yongue, 44.

18. Myra Henshawe must painfully endure the heavy tramping of the Poindexters, a Southern couple who live in the apartment above her. Cather creates a

particularly harsh portrait of the couple. Seen through Myra's eyes they are "The palavery kind of Southerners; all that slushy gush on the surface, and no sensibilities whatever—a race without consonants and without delicacy" (67). The verbal assault on the Poindexters goes on for several pages, leaving us to wonder what Cather had in mind. Quite possibly, in writing of Myra's acknowledgment of her ancestral blood (although Myra's ancestors were Irish), Cather, too, heard the insistent footsteps of the Poindexters overhead, a reminder of her own Southern roots. The negative portrait may well have been Cather's mode of resistance to her own past, particularly since she had chosen to ignore those roots.

19. One of the more interesting autobiographical references is to the picture book Jim and his grandmother make as a Christmas present for Ántonia and Yúlka. They create their book by sewing together squares of cotton cloth for pages, then bind it between pasteboards they have covered with a print "representing scenes from a circus." Jim then cuts pictures from old family magazines that used to publish colored lithographs of popular paintings and pastes them in the book along with "Sunday-School cards and advertising cards," which he says, "I had brought from my 'old country' " (54), meaning, of course, Virginia. The description is an accurate depiction of the Cather family scrapbook, which seems to have been Willa's personal project. The scrapbook, mentioned in Chapter 1, is currently housed in the archives of the Willa Cather Historical Museum, Red Cloud, Nebraska.

20. Paul A. Olson, "*My Ántonia* as Plains Epic," *Approaches to Teaching Cather's My Ántonia,* ed. Susan J. Rosowski (New York: Modern Language Association, 1989), 59.

21. Empson, 15.

22. Ibid.

23. Katrina Irving, "Displacing Homosexuality: The Use of Ethnicity in Willa Cather's *My Ántonia," Modern Fiction Studies* 36 (Spring 1990): 91.

24. Harrison, 9. Harrison's study begins where Annette Kolodny's concludes. She examines the works of twentieth-century Southern women writers to determine if they have been successful at re-visioning the male pastoral plot and establishing an "alternative tradition of their own." See Harrison, 2. For additional information on Kolodny's study of the metaphorical experience of the land-as-woman, see Annette Kolodny, *The Land Before Her: Fantasy and Experience of the American Frontiers, 1630–1860* (Chapel Hill: University of North Carolina Press, 1984), and Kolodny, *The Lay of the Land: Metaphor as Experience and History in American Life and Letters* (Chapel Hill: University of North Carolina Press, 1975).

25. Harrison, 13.

26. Cather was extremely critical of native-born Americans' indifference toward the immigrants, an attitude "especially prevalent among Virginians who . . . looked down on foreigners unless they were English or had titles." See Woodress, 38.

27. Cather's Pulitzer Prize–winning novel *One of Ours* followed *My Ántonia* in 1922, a year before the publication of *A Lost Lady*.

28. The phrases "The Old Order" and "The New Order" are frequently used in reference to the antebellum and postbellum South. The former is associated with an agrarian society, while the latter often refers to the Reconstruction and to the industrialization of the South.

29. Yongue, 119.

30. Cather, too, sought close ties with the immigrants on the Plains and likewise felt just as much at home in the gracious McClung mansion.

31. Bartley Alexander's wife Winifred in *Alexander's Bridge* is also an aristocratic presence, but unlike Marian Forrester, Myra Henshawe, and Sapphira Colbert, she is not a central character in the book.

32. Skaggs, *After the World Broke in Two*, 54.

33. Blanche Gelfant, "The Forgotten Reaping-Hook: Sex in *My Ántonia*," *Critical Essays on Willa Cather*, ed. John J. Murphy (Boston: G. K. Hall & Co., 1984), 149.

34. Mike Fischer, "Pastoralism and Its Discontents: Willa Cather and the Burden of Imperialism," *Mosaic* 23:1 (1990): 31.

35. Paul A. Olson, "The Epic and Great Plains Literature: Rolvaag, Cather, and Neihardt," *Prairie Schooner* 55 (1981): 282.

36. Ibid., 284.

37. *Georgics and Eclogues*, 121.

38. Fischer, 36. Reginald Dyck and others have linked Cather's historical perspective with that of Frederick Jackson Turner, who saw America as entering a state of decline following the postfrontier era, a decline that incorporated the agrarian society as well. See Reginald Dyck, "Revisiting and Revising the West: Willa Cather's *My Ántonia* and Wright Morris' *Plains Song*," *Modern Fiction Studies* 36 (Spring 1990): 37.

39. Fischer, 36.

40. Ibid.

41. Ibid., 37.

42. Woodress, 6.

43. Stouck, *Willa Cather's Imagination*, 46.

44. Toliver, 13.

45. John Murphy, "Willa Cather," *A Literary History of the American West*, sponsored by the Western Literature Association (Fort Worth: Texas Christian University Press, 1987), 691.

46. Simpson, 32–33.

47. Gelfant, 162.

48. Woodress, 348.

49. David Stouck takes the pastoral theme a step further, calling Niel Herbert's

role a "pastoral of experience," presumably intended as the inverse of Poggioli's "pastoral of innocence." Nevertheless, Merrill Maguire Skaggs argues, rightly, I believe, that Niel does not grow, as Stouck suggests, from "childhood innocence to adult awareness and acceptance of life," but instead chooses to deny reality. See Skaggs, *After the World Broke in Two*, 53. See also Stouck, *Willa Cather's Imagination*, 58–59. Woodress makes a similar point: whereas "the dominant theme . . . is the need to reconcile possibility and loss" (a decidedly pastoral theme), it is Marian Forrester, rather than Niel, who comes closest to making this reconciliation. See Woodress, 349.

50. Joseph Urgo sees the novel not as a lament for the past but as an exploration of "the process by which selective events are historicized." See Joseph R. Urgo, "How Context Determines Fact: Historicism in Willa Cather's *A Lost Lady*," *Studies in American Fiction* 17 (1989): 183. See also Joseph R. Urgo, "Historical Movement: What's Lost in *A Lost Lady*," *Novel Frames: Literature as Guide to Race, Sex, and History in American Culture* (Jackson: University of Mississippi Press, 1991), 160–61. Nina Schwartz notes the continuity "between the noble pioneer values and Marian's offense against them, between a glorious past and the fallen present," but contends the novel does not articulate this continuity "in any conscious way. Rather, "it exposes both the mechanisms by which it distorts certain historical actualities and the interest in whose service it operates." See Nina Schwartz, "History and the Invention of Innocence in *A Lost Lady*," *Arizona Quarterly* 46 (Summer 1990): 34.

51. Urgo, "How Context Determines Fact," 189.

52. Schwartz, 47–48.

53. Cather's oft-quoted "the world broke in two in 1922 or thereabouts" suggests a division in her life. See Willa Cather, "Prefatory Note," *Not Under Forty* (Lincoln: University of Nebraska Press, 1922; Bison Book, 1988), v. More than a temporal split—establishing her allegiance to the past rather than the future—the rift was also psychological. O'Brien, Skaggs, Woodress, and others have offered interesting explanations for Cather's mental and emotional state during this time. Whatever the actual cause(s), we know the years between the publication of *One of Ours* in 1922 and the publication of *Death Comes for the Archbishop* were dark ones for the author, as evidenced in the three novels written during that period: *A Lost Lady*, *The Professor's House*, and *My Mortal Enemy*.

54. MacKethan, 4.

55. Reinhold Niebuhr paraphrased in Warren, "The Use of the Past," 34.

56. Warren, "The Use of the Past," 51.

57. Althusser, 169.

58. Stephen Tanner, for example, argues that the ingenuousness of Myra Henshawe's religious conversion negates any possible triumph in her final hours. John Murphy, however, suggests a more positive interpretation of Myra's dubious mo-

tives. See Stephen L. Tanner, "Seeking and Finding in Cather's *My Mortal Enemy*," *Literature and Belief* 8 (1988): 30; and John J. Murphy, "Gilt Diana and Ivory Christ: Love and Christian Charity in *My Mortal Enemy*," *Cather Studies*, vol. 3, ed. Susan J. Rosowski (Lincoln: University of Nebraska Press, 1996), 96–97.

## 4. For Their Own Good: Cather's Pastoral Histories

1. Edward Bloom and Lillian Bloom and James Woodress, among others, give an account of Cather's historical sources, which include: William Joseph Howlett's *The Life of the Right Reverend Joseph P. Machebeuf* (Cather herself mentions this source in her letter to *The Commonweal*) (*WCW* 8), H. H. Bancroft's *History of New Mexico and Arizona*, the works of Charles Lummis, Ralph Emerson Twitchell's *Leading Facts of New Mexico History*, J. B. Salpointe's *Soldiers of the Cross*, Rev. J. H. Defouri's *Historical Sketch of the Catholic Church in New Mexico*, Bandelier's *The Gilded Man*, the *Catholic Encyclopedia*, Francis Palou's *Life of Ven. Padre Junipero Serra*, and the translation of G. P. Winship (in the 14th annual report of the Bureau of American Ethnology) of Castenada's *The Coronado Expedition*. Edward Bloom and Lillian Bloom also offer a partial catalog of the details and events Cather borrowed from Howlett's book. See Edward A. Bloom and Lillian D. Bloom, *Willa Cather's Gift of Sympathy* (Carbondale: Southern Illinois University Press, 1962), 209, 221–28; and Woodress, 393, 403–4.

2. In a youthful essay on Thomas Carlyle, composed when she was only seventeen, Cather wrote: "Art of every kind is an exacting master, more so than even Jehovah. He says only, 'Thou shalt have no other gods before me.' Art, science, and letters cry, 'Thou shalt have no other gods at all.' They accept only human sacrifices." James Woodress contends that Cather embraced this creed throughout her entire artistic career. See Woodress, 74.

3. MacKethan, 5–6.

4. As noted earlier, 1922 and the years that followed had been dark ones for Cather.

5. Shaw defines history as pastoral wherever "history has provided an ideological screen onto which the preoccupations of the present can be projected for clarification and solution, or for disguised expression." See Harry E. Shaw, *The Forms of Historical Fiction: Sir Walter Scott and His Successors* (Ithaca: Cornell University Press, 1983), 52.

6. MacKethan, 4.

7. *I'll Take My Stand: The South and the Agrarian Tradition by Twelve Southerners* (New York: Harper & Brothers, 1930; Harper Torchbook Edition, 1962) includes twelve essays on the preservation of a traditional agrarian South.

8. Although no letters exist (Edith Lewis burned them at Cather's request upon her death) indicating that Cather personally met any of the Agrarians, there

are links that suggest she would have known about their movement. In 1926 and 1927 Allen Tate and his wife Caroline Gordon lived at 27 Bank Street, only a few buildings away from Cather's 5 Bank Street address. Both were acquaintances of Henry Seidel Canby (editor of *The Saturday Review of Literature*) and his wife. Canby, according to Elizabeth Shepley Sergeant, often consulted Cather about new writers he was publishing. Among them was Allen Tate. Moreover, Cather was "deeply aware of post-war life and literary currents." It is more than likely, then, that Cather would have heard about the Southern Agrarian movement and its philosophy. See several references to Canby in *The Literary Correspondence of Donald Davidson and Allen Tate*, ed. John Tyree Fain and Thomas Daniel Young (Athens: University of Georgia Press, 1974). See also Sergeant, *Memoir*, 204, 209.

9. *I'll Take My Stand*, xix.

10. Davidson as quoted in Paul K. Conkin, *The Southern Agrarians* (Knoxville: University of Tennessee Press, 1988), 36.

11. Cather makes several interesting comparative references to the Civil War in *One of Ours*, suggesting her Southern background was never far from her memory. Mahailey observes that atrocities toward women and children were not committed in "our war," i.e., the Civil War. Both her rendition and the narrator's that follows give accounts of Union soldiers behaving civilly and of Mahailey's brothers who fought for the Confederacy (185–86). Mahailey later attempts to understand the purpose of gas masks, something "she hadn't learned about in the Civil War" (200). A reference to Enid's minister Mr. Snowberry, "a simple, courageous man," acknowledges "he had been a drummer boy in the Civil War on the losing side" (165).

12. John Crowe Ransom, "Reconstructed But Unregenerate," *I'll Take My Stand*, 1.

13. Ibid., 3.

14. Ibid., 12.

15. According to Edith Lewis, Cather had been "profoundly interested in Catholicism, especially the Catholicism of the Middle Ages," for most of her life. See Lewis, 147. In 1922, Cather, raised a Southern Baptist, became an Episcopalian and joined the Grace Episcopal Church in Red Cloud.

16. *Literary Correspondence of Donald Davidson and Allen Tate*, 223.

17. Allen Tate, "The Profession of Letters in the South," *Essays of Four Decades* (Chicago: Swallow Press, 1959), 520–21.

18. *Literary Correspondence of Donald Davidson and Allen Tate*, 230.

19. Cather exempts the Americans from this shameful destruction, claiming in a footnote that "the dying pueblo of Pecos was abandoned some years before the American occupation of New Mexico" (123).

20. *Literary Correspondence of Donald Davidson and Allen Tate*, 229–30.

21. As Latour stands before his new Cathedral, wrapped in his Indian blankets

at the end of the novel, he notices the acacia trees in front of the door and thinks "how it was of the South, that Church, how it sounded the note of the South!" (271). Although he is referring to southern France, we are reminded how Cather associated the acacia trees with her childhood in Virginia and wonder at the exclamation point so notable after the word "South," especially given the Old World values that link the two cultures.

22. The exception is Cather's depiction of Kit Carson, whom she greatly admired, although even he is judged for his mistreatment of the Navajo. Bishop Latour recalls how "his own misguided friend, Kit Carson," had been responsible for subduing the last of the Navajo in the Canyon de Chelly (293).

23. Thomas Carlyle, *Past and Present*, vol. X, Edinburgh Edition, The Works of Thomas Carlyle in Thirty Volumes (New York: Charles Scribner's Sons, 1903), 84–89.

24. Carlyle called on his "Captains of Industry" to secure the loyalty of their work forces through benevolent hierarchical structures. "They must and will be regulated, methodically secured in their just share of conquest under you;—joined with you in veritable brotherhood, sonhood, by quite other and deeper ties than those of temporary day wages!" See Carlyle, 274.

25. Ibid., 275.

26. See Ted J. Warner, "*Death Comes for the Archbishop:* A Novel Way of Making History," *Willa Cather: Family, Community, and History* (The BYU Symposium), ed. John J. Murphy (Provo, Utah: Brigham Young University Humanities Publications Center, 1990), 265–73; and Lance Larsen, "Cather's Controversial Portrayal of Martinez," *Willa Cather: Family, Community, and History,* 275–80. For an informative and in-depth analysis of Cather's treatment of history in *Archbishop,* see John Charles Scott, "Between Fiction and History: An Exploration into Willa Cather's *Death Comes for the Archbishop*" (Ph.D. diss., University of New Mexico, 1980).

27. Larsen, 276.

28. Warner, 266. The characters of Jean Marie Latour and Joseph Vaillant are modeled on the lives of Archbishop Jean Baptiste Lamy and Bishop Joseph Machebeuf.

29. Ibid.

30. Warner further contends that along with Cather's violation of historical accuracy, her depiction of Martinez "does considerable damage to the reputation of one of New Mexico's greatest native sons." See Warner, 265.

31. John J. Murphy, "Willa Cather and the Literature of Christian Mystery," *Religion and Literature* 24.3 (Autumn 1992): 47.

32. Ibid.

33. Ibid., 48.

34. According to Edward Bloom and Lillian Bloom, "No authoritative work on the religion and mythology of the Navajos supports [Cather's] position that their gods dwelt in the canyon." See Bloom and Bloom, 216.

35. The belief that it is the "right of the poor and weak to be protected, and of the duty of the rich and strong to protect them," was for Sir Philip Sidney, as Poggioli points out, "one of the chief tasks of the pastoral." See Poggioli, 171.

36. Although David Stouck acknowledges *Shadows on the Rock* as a form of pastoral, he also views it as "preoccupied with the arresting of time and haunted with a vision of impermanence and change." See Stouck, *Willa Cather's Imagination*, 156.

37. Rosowski, 46.

38. Poggioli, 147.

39. Ibid., 157.

40. Skaggs, *After the World Broke in Two*, 128.

41. Lewis, 153.

42. Nisbet, 4.

43. Lewis, 155–56.

44. Empson, 87.

45. Carlyle, 275.

46. E. K. Brown, 308.

47. For in-depth discussions on Cather's employment of Parkman's histories in *Shadows*, see Merrill Maguire Skaggs, "Cather's Use of Parkman's Histories in *Shadows on the Rock*," *Cather Studies*, vol. 2, ed. Susan J. Rosowski (Lincoln: University of Nebraska Press, 1993), and Gary Brienzo, *Willa Cather's Transforming Vision: New France and the American Northeast* (Selinsgrove, PA: Susquehanna University Press, 1994).

48. Wilbur R. Jacobs, "Willa Cather and Francis Parkman: Novelistic Portrayals of Colonial New France," *Willa Cather: Family, Community, and History* (The BYU Symposium), ed. John J. Murphy (Provo, Utah: Brigham Young University Humanities Publications Center, 1990), 254.

49. Ibid., 260.

50. Ibid., 259.

51. Ibid.

52. Lewis, 119.

53. Simpson, 69.

54. Cather's eleventh novel, *Lucy Gayheart*, was written between these two novels and published in 1935.

55. The "garden of the chattel," as noted earlier, is a phrase created by Louis P. Simpson. See Simpson, 2.

## 5. History and Memory: Cather's Garden of the Chattel

1. According to Lewis P. Simpson, the Southern Literary Renaissance has two major stages, the first of which took place from the early 1920s to about 1950, the second from after World War II to the present. All references to the Southern Renaissance in this study refer only to the first major stage. See Simpson, 70.

2. As Jo Ann Middleton points out, returning to the past was a common literary device for modernist writers as well. While the writers of the Southern Renaissance chose to examine their own antebellum past, as Cather does in *Sapphira*, modernists, however, usually "returned to a more exotic or primitive culture, or of a classic Greek and Roman myth, as Cather does when she returns to the pre-European, native American past." See Middleton, 10–11.

3. Simpson, 70.

4. "The Uses of History in Fiction," A panel discussion by Ralph Ellison, William Styron, Robert Penn Warren, C. Vann Woodward, *The Southern Literary Journal* 1 (1969): 61.

5. Granville Hicks, "The Case against Willa Cather," *Willa Cather and Her Critics*, ed. James Schroeter (Ithaca, NY: Cornell University Press, 1967), 144.

6. Cleanth Brooks, "The Past Alive in the Present," *American Letters and the Historical Consciousness*, ed. J. Gerald Kennedy and Daniel Mark Fogel (Baton Rouge: Louisiana State University Press, 1987), 217.

7. Richard M. Weaver, *The Southern Tradition at Bay: A History of Postbellum Thought* (New Rochelle, NY: Arlington House, 1968), 341.

8. Merrill Maguire Skaggs argues convincingly that Cather undertook the writing of *Sapphira* in response to her critics, particularly Granville Hicks who accused her of succumbing to "supine romanticism." Thus Cather set out intentionally to subvert readers' cultural expectations by reversing stereotypical elements. Skaggs, *After the World Broke in Two*, 167–68, 170–71.

9. Willa Cather to Dorothy Canfield Fisher, 14 October 1940, Guy Bailey Memorial Library, University of Vermont. See also Stouck, *Willa Cather's Imagination*, 226.

10. Willa Cather to Viola Roseboro, 9 November 1940 and 28 November 1940, The Barrett Collection, University of Virginia. See also Marilyn Arnold, " 'Of Human Bondage': Cather's Subnarrative in *Sapphira and the Slave Girl*," *Mississippi Quarterly* 40 (1987): 323.

11. Stouck, *Willa Cather's Imagination*, 227–28.

12. Skaggs, *After the World Broke in Two*, 176.

13. Ibid., 169–70. For a discussion on stereotypical characters in Southern local color fiction, see Skaggs, *Folk of Southern Fiction*, 141–53.

14. For a further discussion on Cather's reversal of African American stereo-

types in *Sapphira*, see Loretta Wasserman, "*Sapphira and the Slave Girl:* Willa Cather vs Margaret Mitchell," *Willa Cather Pioneer Memorial Newsletter* 38 (Spring 1994): 1–15.

15. Hermione Lee also sees evidence of the pastoral in the seasonal labor. See Lee, 361. The labor, however, and therefore the pastoral element, is associated with the Miller and the Mill Farm slaves. Sapphira, in her present state, does not share in the connection to the land.

16. Williams, 17.

17. According to Lewis Simpson, the concept of the "plantation as a homeland of the life of the mind" is derived from the pastoral vision of Western culture. If the plantation signifies pastoral social order, "the fear of slavery" is "not simply a threat to the social order but to "the very source of order—that is, the mind and imagination." See Simpson, 23.

18. Ibid., 30.

19. Ibid.

20. Thomas Jefferson, *Notes on the State of Virginia*, ed. William Peden (Chapel Hill: University of North Carolina Press, 1955), 164–65.

21. William Gilmore Simms, perhaps the antebellum South's most prominent author, once considered leaving the South out of despair for the independent artist. "Here I am nothing & can be & can do nothing. The South don't care a d——n for literature or art. Your best neighbor & kindred never think to buy books. They will borrow from you & beg, but the same man who will always have his wine, has no idea of a library. You will write for & defend their institutions in vain. They will not pay the expense of printing your essays." *The Letters of William Gilmore Simms*, ed. Mary C. Simms Oliphant et al., Vol. II (Columbia: University of South Carolina Press, 1953), 386.

22. An absence of aesthetic sensibility, for Cather, is concomitant with the lack of spirituality. In Cather's letter to Michael Williams in the *Commonweal* regarding escapism, she reminds him that "Religion and art spring from the same root and are close kin. Economics and art are strangers" (*WCW* 27). Moreover, the absence of both negates any true "aristocratic" dimension in Sapphira's nature. But as Merrill Maguire Skaggs notes, Sapphira's character is intended "to undermine the stereotype of the Southern aristocrat." See Skaggs, *After the World Broke in Two*, 173, 207, n. 8.

23. Cather's maternal grandmother, Caroline Cather, was descended from Jeremiah Smith, who came to Virginia from England in the early 1700s and, like Nathaniel Dodderidge, was deeded land on Back Creek by Lord Fairfax. See Woodress, 15.

24. Woodward, 62.

25. Simms's response to Harriet Martineau's *Society in America*. His response

was published in the Richmond *Southern Literary Messenger* III (November 1837), 653. The italics are Simms's. His arguments are hardly new and were the standard propaganda of that era. Cather, "having grown up with a special interest in the writers of the South," and being an avid reader of Simms's protégé John Esten Cooke (*KA* 41) would have been familiar with these contentions.

26. Ibid., 657.

27. The Pottawatomie massacre, which took place in Kansas on 24 May 1856, resulted in a raid on four proslavery families, none of which actually owned slaves. Brown justified his bloody deeds—raiding the homes and systematically executing five men (two of whom had been born in Germany) and leaving their "bodies horribly mutilated"—by claiming his actions had been "decreed by Almighty God, ordained from Eternity." While hardly an act that would have united him with intelligent opponents of slavery, he nevertheless went on to acquire a considerable following. After the Harper's Ferry uprising, his supporters would include Emerson and Longfellow. See Woodward, 43, 54. Brown's exploits were well known to Virginians. Cather's family, too, would have been familiar with these stories, particularly since they took place in her parents' lifetime.

28. Ibid., 62.

29. Ibid., 42.

30. Cather earlier used a phonetic spelling to hint likewise at M(yra) Henshaw's rage in *My Mortal Enemy.*

31. Willa Cather to Viola Roseboro, 20 February 1941, The Barrett Collection, University of Virginia.

32. Henry Seidel Canby, "Conversation Piece," *Saturday Review of Literature* 23 (14 December 1940), 5.

33. Simms, in *Southern Literary Messenger,* 657.

34. As Mary W. Stewart argued during her speech in the Boston African Masonic Hall in 1833: "so also have the white Americans gained themselves a name . . . while in reality we have been their principle foundation and support. We have pursued the shadow, they have obtained the substance; we have performed the labor, they have received the profits; we have planted the vines, they have eaten the fruits of them . . . " See M. W. Stewart, "Throw Off Your Fearfullness and Come Forth," *Black Women in White America: A Documentary History,* ed. G. Lerner (New York, 1972), 529.

35. Toni Morrison questions the logic of the arranged rape of Nancy, and how it would deter Henry Colbert's interest in her, since the outcome would seem to make her more easily accessible to him. See Toni Morrison, *Playing in the Dark: Whiteness and the Literary Imagination* (Cambridge: Harvard University Press, 1992), 25. Deborah Carlin suggests that the story is "not really about the condition of African Americans in slavery, but about the way (white) versions of history *need*

to remember and to represent black people in order to maintain a political, economic, and social hierarchy." See Deborah Carlin, *Cather, Canon, and the Politics of Reading* (Amherst: University of Massachusetts Press, 1992), 176. Ultimately, this is not a story about Nancy but about how she is perceived by different members of a white household, all of whom hold opposing views on the issue of slavery.

36. Lewis Simpson makes an intriguing case for Poe's "The Fall of the House of Usher" as a symbolic anticipation of the self-destruction of the antebellum aristocracy. See Simpson, 67–69.

37. Toni Morrison contends that it is difficult to believe Till would turn her back on her daughter under such conditions. "That condition could only prevail in a slave society where the mistress can count on (and an author can believe the reader does not object to) the complicity of a mother in the seduction and rape of her own daughter." See Morrison, 21.

38. William Faulkner, *The Sound and the Fury* (New York: Random House, Vintage Books, 1956), 427.

39. Sergeant, *Memoir,* 280.

40. Minrose C. Gwin, *Black and White Women of the Old South: The Peculiar Sisterhood in American Literature* (Knoxville: University of Tennessee Press, 1985), 135.

41. C. Hugh Holman, *The Immoderate Past: The Southern Writer and History* (Athens: University of Georgia Press, 1977), 16.

42. Woodress, 488.

43. Ibid., 485.

44. Ibid.

45. Morrison, 28.

46. Woodress, 493.

47. Ibid.

48. Lewis, 183.

# Bibliography

## Works by Willa Cather

*Alexander's Bridge*. New York: New American Library, A Meridian Classic, 1988.

*April Twilights* (1903). Edited with an introduction by Bernice Slote. Lincoln: University of Nebraska Press, 1962.

*April Twilights and Other Poems*. New York: Alfred A. Knopf, A Borzoi Book, 1923.

*Death Comes for the Archbishop*. New York: Alfred A. Knopf, 1927; reprint, New York: Random House, Vintage Books, 1971.

*The Kingdom of Art: Willa Cather's First Principles and Critical Statements, 1893–1896*. Edited by Bernice Slote. Lincoln: University of Nebraska Press, 1966.

*A Lost Lady*. New York: Alfred A. Knopf, 1923; reprint, New York: Random House, Vintage Books, 1972.

*Lucy Gayheart*. New York: Alfred A. Knopf, 1935; reprint, New York: Random House, Vintage Books, 1976.

*My Ántonia*. Boston: Houghton Mifflin, 1918; paperback edition, 1977.

*My Mortal Enemy*. New York: Alfred A. Knopf, 1926; reprint, New York: Random House, Vintage Books, 1954.

*Not Under Forty*. New York: Alfred A. Knopf, 1922; reprint, Lincoln: University of Nebraska Press, Bison Book, 1988.

*Obscure Destinies*. New York: Alfred A. Knopf, 1932; reprint, New York: Random House, Vintage Books, 1974.

*The Old Beauty and Others*. New York: Alfred A. Knopf, 1948; reprint, New York: Random House, Vintage Books, 1976.

*One of Ours*. New York: Alfred A. Knopf, 1922; reprint, New York: Random House, Vintage Books, 1971.

*O Pioneers!* Boston: Houghton Mifflin, 1913; paperback edition, 1988.

*The Professor's House*. New York: Alfred A. Knopf, 1925; reprint, New York: Random House, Vintage Books, 1973.

*Sapphira and the Slave Girl*. New York: Alfred A. Knopf, 1940; reprint, New York: Random House, Vintage Books, 1975.

*Shadows on the Rock*. New York: Alfred A. Knopf, 1931; reprint, New York: Random House, Vintage Books, 1971.

*The Song of the Lark.* Boston: Houghton Mifflin, 1915; paperback edition, 1988.

*The Troll Garden.* New York: New American Library, A Meridian Classic, 1984.

*Uncle Valentine and Other Stories: Willa Cather's Uncollected Short Fiction 1915–1929.* Edited with an introduction by Bernice Slote. Lincoln: University of Nebraska Press, Bison Book, 1986.

*Willa Cather: A Biographical Sketch/ An English Opinion/ and an Abridged Bibliography.* New York: Alfred A. Knopf, n.d.

*Willa Cather in Person: Interviews, Speeches, and Letters.* Edited by L. Brent Bohlke. Lincoln: University of Nebraska Press, 1986, Bison Book, 1990.

*Willa Cather on Writing: Critical Studies on Writing as an Art.* New York: Alfred A. Knopf, 1920; reprint, Lincoln: University of Nebraska Press, Bison Book, 1988.

*Willa Cather's Collected Short Fiction, 1892–1912.* Edited by Virginia Faulkner. Lincoln: University of Nebraska Press, 1965; revised edition, 1970.

*The World and the Parish: Willa Cather's Articles and Reviews, 1893–1902.* Vol. I and II. Edited by William M. Curtin. Lincoln: University of Nebraska Press, 1970.

*Youth and the Bright Medusa.* New York: Alfred A. Knopf, 1920; reprint, New York: Random House, Vintage Books, 1975.

### Letters

The Barrett Collection, University of Virginia, Charlottesville, Virginia.

    Willa Cather to Mrs. Ackroyd, 16 May 1941.

    Willa Cather to Viola Roseboro, 9 November 1940, 28 November 1940, 20 February 1941.

Guy Bailey Memorial Library, University of Vermont, Burlington, Vermont.

    Willa Cather to Dorothy Canfield Fisher, 14 October 1940.

Willa Cather Memorial Museum, Red Cloud, Nebraska.

    Willa Cather to Mariel Gere, 1 August 1893, June or July 1896.

### Other Works

Althusser, Louis. "Ideology and Ideological State Apparatuses (Notes towards an investigation)." *Lenin and Philosophy and Other Essays.* Translated by Ben Brewster, 127–86. New York: Monthly Review Press, 1971.

Ammons, Elizabeth. "Art: Willa Cather, the Woman Writer as Artist, and Humishuma." *Conflicting Stories: American Women Writers at the Turn into the Twentieth Century.* New York: Oxford University Press, 1991.

Arnold, Marilyn. " 'Of Human Bondage': Cather's Subnarrative *Sapphira and the Slave Girl.*" *Mississippi Quarterly* 40 (1987).

———. *Willa Cather's Short Fiction.* Athens: Ohio University Press, 1984; paperback edition, 1986.

Bennett, Mildred. "The Childhood Worlds of Willa Cather." *Great Plains Quarterly* 2.4 (1982): 204–9.

———. *The World of Willa Cather.* New York: Dodd, Mead and Company, 1951.

Bloom, Edward A., and Lillian D. Bloom. *Willa Cather's Gift of Sympathy.* Carbondale: Southern Illinois University Press, 1962.

Brienzo, Gary. *Willa Cather's Transforming Vision: New France and the American Northeast.* Selinsgrove, PA: Susquehanna University Press, 1994.

Brooks, Cleanth. "The Past Alive in the Present." *American Letters and the Historical Consciousness.* Edited by J. Gerald Kennedy and Daniel Mark Fogel, 1–14. Baton Rouge: Louisiana State University Press, 1987.

Brown, E. K. *Willa Cather: A Critical Biography.* Completed by Leon Edel. New York: Alfred A. Knopf, 1953; reprint, Lincoln: University of Nebraska Press, Bison Book, 1987.

Brown, Virginia Verle (Lady Falls). "Willa Cather and the Southern Genteel Tradition." Ph.D. diss. Texas Tech University, 1989.

Callander, Marilyn Berg. *Willa Cather and the Fairy Tale.* Ann Arbor, MI: UMI Research Press, 1989.

Canby, Henry Seidel. "Conversation Piece." *Saturday Review of Literature* 23 (14 December 1940).

Carlin, Deborah. *Cather, Canon, and the Politics of Reading.* Amherst: University of Massachusetts Press, 1992.

Carlyle, Thomas. *Past and Present.* Vol. X. Edinburgh Edition, The Works of Thomas Carlyle in Thirty Volumes. New York: Charles Scribner's Sons, 1903.

Cash, W. J. *The Mind of the South.* New York: Alfred A. Knopf, 1941.

Conkin, Paul K. *The Southern Agrarians.* Knoxville: University of Tennessee Press, 1988.

Donovan, Josephine. *After the Fall: The Demeter-Persephone Myth in Wharton, Cather, and Glasgow.* University Park: Pennsylvania State University Press, 1989.

Drayton, Michael. *The Works of Michael Drayton.* Vol. II. Edited by J. William Hebel. New York: Oxford University Press, 1931.

Dyck, Reginald. "Revisiting and Revising the West: Willa Cather's *My Ántonia* and Wright Morris' *Plains Song.*" *Modern Fiction Studies* 36:1 (Spring 1990): 25–38.

Empson, William. *Some Versions of Pastoral.* London: Chatto & Windus, 1935.

Faulkner, William. *Light in August.* Harrison Smith and Robert Haas, 1932; reprint, New York: Random House, Vintage Books, 1972.

———. *The Sound and the Fury.* 1930. New York: Random House, Vintage Books, 1956.

Fischer, Mike. "Pastoralism and Its Discontents: Willa Cather and the Burden of Imperialism." *Mosaic* 23:1 (1990): 31–44.

Gaines, Francis Pendleton. *The Southern Plantation: A Study in the Development and the Accuracy of a Tradition.* New York: Columbia University Press, 1924; Gloucester, MA: Peter Smith, 1962.

Gelfant, Blanche. "The Forgotten Reaping-Hook: Sex in *My Ántonia.*" *Critical Essays on Willa Cather.* Edited by John J. Murphy, 147–64. Boston: G. K. Hall & Co., 1984.

Gray, Richard. *The Literature of Memory: Modern Writers of the American South.* Baltimore: Johns Hopkins University Press, 1977.

Gwin, Minrose C. *Black and White Women of the Old South: The Peculiar Sisterhood in American Literature.* Knoxville: University of Tennessee Press, 1985.

Harrell, David. *From Mesa Verde to The Professor's House.* Albuquerque: University of New Mexico Press, 1992.

Harrison, Elizabeth Jane. *Female Pastoral: Women Writers Re-Visioning the American South.* Knoxville: University of Tennessee Press, 1991.

Hicks, Granville. "The Case against Willa Cather." *Willa Cather and Her Critics,* ed. James Schroeter. Ithaca, NY: Cornell University Press, 1967.

Holman, C. Hugh. *The Immoderate Past: The Southern Writer and History.* The 1976 Lamar Lectures at Wesleyan College. Athens: University of Georgia Press, 1977.

———. *The Roots of Southern Writing: Essays on the Literature of the American South.* Athens: University of Georgia Press, 1972.

*I'll Take My Stand: The South and the Agrarian Tradition by Twelve Southerners.* New York: Harper & Brothers, 1930; Harper Torchbook Edition, 1962.

Irving, Katrina. "Displacing Homosexuality: The Use of Ethnicity in Willa Cather's *My Ántonia.*" *Modern Fiction Studies* 36.1 (Spring 1990): 91–102.

Jacobs, Wilbur R. "Willa Cather and Francis Parkman: Novelistic Portrayals of Colonial New France." *Willa Cather: Family, Community, and History.* The BYU Symposium. Edited by John J. Murphy, 253–64. Provo, Utah: Brigham Young University Humanities Publications Center, 1990.

Jefferson, Thomas. *Notes on the State of Virginia.* Edited by William Peden. Chapel Hill: University of North Carolina Press, 1955.

Kolodny, Annette. *The Land Before Her: Fantasy and Experience of the American Frontiers, 1630–1860.* Chapel Hill: University of North Carolina Press, 1984.

———. *The Lay of the Land: Metaphor as Experience and History in American Life and Letters.* Chapel Hill: University of North Carolina Press, 1975.

Larsen, Lance. "Cather's Controversial Portrayal of Martinez." *Willa Cather: Family, Community, and History.* The BYU Symposium. Edited by John J. Murphy, 275–80. Provo, Utah: Brigham Young University Humanities Publications Center, 1990.

Lee, Hermione. *Willa Cather: Double Lives.* New York: Pantheon Books, 1989.

Lewis, Edith. *Willa Cather Living: A Personal Record.* New York: Alfred A. Knopf, 1953.

*The Literary Correspondence of Donald Davidson and Allen Tate.* Edited by John Tyree Fain and Thomas Daniel Young. Athens: University of Georgia Press, 1974.

MacKethan, Lucinda Hardwick. *The Dream of Arcady: Place and Time in Southern Literature.* Baton Rouge: Louisiana State University Press, 1980.

Marambaud, Pierre. *William Byrd of Westover, 1674–1744.* Charlottesville: University Press of Virginia, 1971.

Marx, Leo. *The Machine in the Garden: Technology and the Pastoral Ideal in America.* New York: Oxford University Press, 1964.

Middleton, Jo Ann. *Willa Cather's Modernism: A Study of Style and Technique.* Rutherford, NJ: Fairleigh Dickinson University Press, 1990.

Moers, Ellen. "Comment." *The Art of Willa Cather.* Edited by Bernice Slote and Virginia Faulkner. Lincoln: University of Nebraska Press, 1974.

Morrison, Toni. *Playing in the Dark: Whiteness and the Literary Imagination.* Cambridge: Harvard University Press, 1992.

Murphy, John J. "Gilt Diana and Ivory Christ: Love and Christian Charity in *My Mortal Enemy*." *Cather Studies,* Vol. 3. Edited by Susan J. Rosowski. Lincoln: University of Nebraska Press, 1996.

———. "The Missions of Latour and Paul: *Death Comes for the Archbishop* and the Early Church." *Literature and Belief* 8 (1988): 58–65.

———. *My Ántonia: The Road Home.* Twayne's Masterwork Studies 31. Boston: Twayne Publishers, 1989.

———. "Willa Cather." *A Literary History of the American West,* sponsored by the Western Literature Association, 686–715. Fort Worth: Texas Christian University Press, 1987.

———. "Willa Cather and the Literature of Christian Mystery." *Religion and Literature* 24.3 (1992): 39–56.

Nisbet, Robert A. *Tradition and Revolt: Historical and Sociological Essays.* New York: Random House, 1968.

O'Brien, Sharon. *Willa Cather: The Emerging Voice.* New York: Oxford University Press, 1987; reprint, New York: Ballantine Books, A Fawcett Columbine Book, 1987.

Olson, Paul A. "The Epic and Great Plains Literature: Rolvaag, Cather, and Neihardt. *Prairie Schooner* 55 (1981).

———. "*My Ántonia* as Plains Epic." *Approaches to Teaching Cather's My Ántonia.* Edited by Susan J. Rosowski. New York: Modern Language Association, 1989.

Parkman, Francis. *France and England in North America.* Vol. 1. Library of America Edition. New York: Literary Classics of the United States, 1983.

———. *France and England in North America.* Vol. 2. Library of America Edition. New York: Literary Classics of the United States, 1983.

Parry, Susan. "The Cather Home Place: Willow Shade in Memory and Reality."

Paper read at the Fifth International Willa Cather Seminar, 19–26 June 1993, at Hastings College, Hastings, Nebraska.

Poggioli, Renato. "The Oaten Flute." *Harvard Literary Bulletin* 11 (1957): 147–84.

Randall, John H., III. *The Landscape and the Looking Glass: Willa Cather's Search for Value.* Westport, CT: Greenwood, 1960.

———. "Willa Cather and the Pastoral Tradition." *Five Essays on Willa Cather: The Merrimack Symposium.* Edited by John J. Murphy, 75–96. North Andover, MA: Merrimack College, 1974.

Ransom, John Crowe. "Reconstructed But Unregenerate." *I'll Take My Stand: The South and the Agrarian Tradition by Twelve Southerners,* 1–27. New York: Harper & Brothers, Harper Torchbook Edition, 1962.

Ridgely, J. V. *William Gilmore Simms.* New York: Twayne Publishers, 1962.

Robinson, Phyllis C. *Willa: The Life of Willa Cather.* Garden City, NY: Doubleday & Company, 1983.

Romines, Ann. *The Home Plot: Women, Writing & Domestic Ritual.* Amherst: University of Massachusetts Press, 1992.

Rosowski, Susan J. *The Voyage Perilous: Willa Cather's Romanticism.* Lincoln: University of Nebraska Press, 1986.

Ryder, Mary Ruth. *Willa Cather and Classical Myth: The Search for a New Parnassus.* Studies in American Literature 11. Lewiston, NY: Edwin Mellen Press, 1990.

Schwartz, Nina. "History and the Invention of Innocence in *A Lost Lady.*" *Arizona Quarterly* 46.2 (1990): 33–54.

Scott, John Charles. "Between Fiction and History: An Exploration into Willa Cather's *Death Comes for the Archbishop.*" Ph.D. diss. University of New Mexico, 1980.

Sergeant, Elizabeth Shepley. "Willa Cather." *The New Republic.* 17 June 1925.

———. *Willa Cather: A Memoir.* Philadelphia: Lippincott, 1953; reprint, Athens: Ohio University Press, 1992.

Shaw, Harry E. *The Forms of Historical Fiction: Sir Walter Scott and His Successors.* Ithaca: Cornell University Press, 1983.

Simms, William Gilmore. *The Letters of William Gilmore Simms.* Collected and edited by Mary C. Simms Oliphant et al. Vol II. Columbia: University of South Carolina Press, 1953.

———. (n.t.) *Southern Literary Messenger* III (November 1837): 641–57.

Simpson, Lewis P. *The Dispossessed Garden: Pastoral and History in Southern Literature.* Mercer University Lamar Memorial Lectures, 16. Athens: University of Georgia Press, 1975.

Skaggs, Merrill Maguire. *After the World Broke in Two: The Later Novels of Willa Cather.* Charlottesville: University Press of Virginia, 1990.

———. "Cather's Use of Parkman's Histories in *Shadows on the Rock.*" *Cather Stud-*

*ies.* Vol. 2. Edited by Susan J. Rosowski, 140–55. Lincoln: University of Nebraska Press, 1993.

——. *The Folk of Southern Fiction.* Athens: University of Georgia Press, 1972.

——. "Teaching 'Old Mrs. Harris.'" *Nebraska English Journal* 37.1 (1991): 75–84.

——. "Willa Cather's Experimental Southern Novel." *Mississippi Quarterly* 35.1 (1981–82): 3–14.

Skinner, Tina. "Freed Slaves Found Mecca in Local Area." *Winchester Star.* 1 February 1992.

Slote, Bernice. "First Principles: The Kingdom of Art." *The Kingdom of Art: Willa Cather's First Principles and Critical Statements, 1893–1896.* Edited by Bernice Slote, 31–112. Lincoln: University of Nebraska Press, 1966.

——. "Introduction." *Uncle Valentine and Other Stories: Willa Cather's Uncollected Short Fiction, 1915–1929.* Edited by Bernice Slote, ix–xxx. Lincoln: University of Nebraska Press, 1973.

Stewart, M. W. "Throw Off Your Fearfullness and Come Forth." *Black Women in White America: A Documentary History.* Edited by G. Lerner. New York, 1972.

Stouck, David. "Willa Cather and the Indian Heritage." *Twentieth Century Literature* 22 (1976): 433–43.

——. *Willa Cather's Imagination.* Lincoln: University of Nebraska Press, 1975.

Stout, Janis P. *Strategies of Reticence: Silence and Meaning in the Works of Jane Austen, Willa Cather, Katherine Anne Porter, and Joan Didion.* Charlottesville: University Press of Virginia, 1990.

Tanner, Stephen L. "Seeking and Finding in Cather's *My Mortal Enemy.*" *Literature and Belief* 8 (1988).

Tate, Allen. "The Profession of Letters in the South." *Essays of Four Decades.* Chicago: Swallow Press, 1959.

Taylor, William R. *Cavalier and Yankee: The Old South and American National Character.* New York: George Braziller, 1961.

Toliver, Harold E. *Pastoral Forms and Attitudes.* Berkeley: University of California Press, 1971.

Urgo, Joseph R. "How Context Determines Fact: Historicism in Willa Cather's *A Lost Lady.*" *Studies in American Fiction* 17.2 (1989): 183–92.

——. *Novel Frames: Literature as Guide to Race, Sex, and History in American Culture.* Jackson: University Press of Mississippi, 1991.

——. *Willa Cather and the Myth of American Migration.* Urbana and Chicago: University of Illinois Press, 1995.

"The Uses of History in Fiction." A panel discussion by Ralph Ellison, William Styron, Robert Penn Warren, C. Vann Woodward. *The Southern Literary Journal* 1 (1969): 57–90.

Virgil. *The Georgics and Eclogues of Virgil.* Translated by Theodore Chickering Williams. Cambridge: Harvard University Press, 1915.

Warner, Ted J. "*Death Comes for the Archbishop:* A Novel Way of Making History." *Willa Cather: Family, Community, and History.* The BYU Symposium. Edited by John J. Murphy, 265–73. Provo, Utah: Brigham Young University Humanities Publications Center, 1990.

Warren, Robert Penn. *All the King's Men.* San Diego: Harcourt Brace Jovanovich, 1946; A Harvest/HBJ Book, 1982.

———. *The Legacy of the Civil War.* New York: Random House, 1961; reprint, Cambridge: Harvard University Press, 1983.

———. "The Use of the Past." *New and Selected Essays.* New York: Random House, 1989.

Wasserman, Loretta. "*Sapphira and the Slave Girl:* Willa Cather vs Margaret Mitchell." *Willa Cather Pioneer Memorial Newsletter* 38.1 (Spring 1994): 1–15.

———. *Willa Cather: A Study of the Short Fiction.* Twayne's Studies in Short Fiction Series 19. Boston: Twayne Publishers, 1991.

Weaver, Richard M. *The Southern Tradition at Bay: A History of Postbellum Thought.* New Rochelle, NY: Arlington House, 1968.

Welty, Eudora. "The House of Willa Cather." *The Eye of the Story: Selected Essays and Reviews,* 41–60. New York: Random House, 1977.

Whitman, Walt. *Leaves of Grass.* Norton Critical Edition. Edited by Sculley Bradley and Harold W. Blodgett. New York: Oxford University Press, 1973.

Williams, Raymond. *The Country and the City.* New York: Oxford University Press, 1973.

Winters, Laura. *Willa Cather: Landscape and Exile.* Selinsgrove, PA: Susquehanna University Press, 1993.

Wister, Owen. *The Virginian: A Horseman of the Plains.* New York: Macmillan Company, 1902.

Woodress, James. *Willa Cather: A Literary Life.* Lincoln: University of Nebraska Press, 1987; Bison Book, 1989.

Woodward, C. Vann. *The Burden of Southern History.* Baton Rouge: Louisiana State University Press, 1960.

Yongue, Patricia Lee. "Willa Cather's Aristocrats" (Part I and Part II). *Southern Humanities Review* 14 (1980): 43–56, 111–25.

# Index